Explosive Litigation

HOW TO MASTER THE CASES
AND DOMINATE THE COURTROOM

SAMUEL PARTIDA, JR.

Copyright © 2018 Samuel Partida, Jr.
All rights reserved.
ISBN: 1985797992
ISBN-13: 9781985797994

DEDICATION

To Barbara Partida, my beautiful and patient wife who is waiting for me to get my act together.

TABLE OF CONTENTS

Dedication	2
Acknowledgments	7
Bonus Episodes	8

Section One: Tech & The Law — 10
What's In This Book — 12

Section Two: Court Embarrassment — 14
First D'Oh Moment — 15
Second D'Oh Moment — 16

Section Three: Why Podcasts Work — 18
Designed To Fail — 18
Flip The Cases — 20
How The Brain Works — 23
Audio Learning For Lawyers — 29

Section Four: DUI Roadblocks — 31
DUI Roadblock Foundation (People v. Ray) — 32
Illinois v. Lidster — 34
People v. Bartley — 37
Answer The Top 10 Questions — 42

Section Five: The Meaning Of Proof Beyond A Reasonable Doubt   52
Illinois Is Different   52
People v. Downs   55
People v. Thomas   58
People v. Franklin   59
What To Tell The Jury   60

Section Six: The Krankel Two-Step   62
People v. Krankel   62
People v. Flemming   64
People v. Boose   69
People v. Ayres   75
People v. Brown   78

Section Seven: Double Jeopardy Tips, Tricks And Litigation Tactics   85
People v. Guillen   86
People v. Staple   99
People v. Threatte   105
People v. Kimball   113
Final Tip On Litigating Double Jeopardy Issues   123

Section Eight: The Surveillance Privilege   125
People v. Flournoy   125
In re Manuel   132
People v. Palmer   136
People v. Jackson   143

Section Nine: The Limitations Of Print   150

ACKNOWLEDGMENTS

To all the current subscribers to the Premium Nuggets Podcast, thank you. You are dedicated professionals active in improving criminal justice. Your discovery that you can use your ears to advance your practice has made this adventure possible.

BONUS EPISODES

I packaged together and made available for download some bonus podcast episodes. These episodes are available for FREE just for readers of this book. I have not made these episodes available anywhere else. Any person with an interest in the criminal law will find these downloads useful. Go here to get them now:

https://IllinoisCaseLaw.com/book-bonus

SECTION ONE: TECH & THE LAW

I'm constantly looking around at the fast-paced changes in technology and asking if any of that stuff can help me.

I'm a human and a criminal law lawyer. So I've taken advantage of the internet, communication, and media advancements occuring in my lifetime. In the legal community there is also a lot of talk with buzz words like "legal tech." As a criminal law attorney, I often find most of those "legal tech" ideas lacking in any criminal law applications.

I am aware of revolutionary systems used by the various circuit clerks to go "paperless." Applications that help me and my colleagues to be better criminal law litigators just aren't there.

As a result, I just tune out when I hear about some new gadget or website that's going to "revolutionize" the law as we know it. Attorneys in the criminal law game have different problems to worry about. Problems like putting a dent in all the wrongful convictions passing through the system, problems like keeping up with all the latest changes in the law and in the cases, problems like making sure we're on our toes in court and making sure the other side is not trying to pull one over on us, problems like mastering trial techniques. Where's the tech that will stop us from embarrassing ourselves in court?

When a technology comes along that can help with these issues, that's when I'll stand up and take notice. So far, though, I ain't been impressed...

Then I discovered podcasts. I got started listening to podcasts in 2008. That was when we saw the problem in the housing market, and we fluttered with a modern day depression. Naturally, I searched for sources that could help me understand what the hell was going on.

I found a podcast by an economist at George Mason. His name was Russ Roberts and his podcast was called EconTalk. I don't have any economic training whatsoever, but I thought Russ did a great job of breaking down complicated ideas and talking about them in a conversational level that anyone could understand.

Then I discovered all kinds of other podcasts. There were fun ones, entertaining ones, silly ones. In general, I thought they were all a big waste of time.

Out of guilt, I started looking around for the podcast that would help me be a better Illinois criminal law attorney. I just assumed that some smart, technologically-oriented attorney had started the podcast for criminal law litigators.

I found no shortage of legal podcasts, but none of them really helped solve any of the problems I addressed above. None of the podcasts were produced for Illinois criminal law attorneys.

That's when I decided that if this mythical podcast for me and my colleagues was ever going to be created, I probably had to be the one to do it.

WHAT'S IN THIS BOOK

In this book, I'll tell you two short stories that illuminate the basic problems criminal litigators confront in court. Also, I'll explain why a podcast for Illinois criminal law attorneys is the best tech on the market right now that helps address these problems.

This just can't be any legal podcast. To be effective, a podcast for litigators has to be tailored made for a niche audience. If a podcast can get into the nitty gritty of an Illinois courtroom, then it can begin to truly revolutionize the spread of knowledge and ideas. This kind of learning isn't unique to my kind of law. Niche-specific podcasts will work beautifully in most technical and academic fields if someone takes the time to produce them.

In the remainder of this book, I'll discuss five areas in the Illinois criminal law that serve as great examples of the legal learning that occurred because of a podcast. I'll discuss five subjects in the Illinois law that I recorded episodes about. These are five subjects that my audience of Illinois criminal attorneys didn't have to invest time to hunt down, read, and digest. These were five areas of the Illinois criminal law that were used by the listeners to be better in court, made them better litigators, and helped them stay sharp against the opposition.

The cool part is that they got the benefit of knowledge and experience by listening to the information rather than reading it. The five issues that I'll discuss deal with:

- DUI Roadblocks
- Reasonable Doubt
- Krankel Inquiries
- Double Jeopardy
- Surveillance Privilege

In the substantive parts of this book I have included links to specific podcast episodes that you can listen to if you happen to have a browser handy. Some of the podcasts were recorded when I was first getting started with podcasting, so don't be too hard on me.

I'm going to sound extremely nervous and unsure about myself. That's because I was extremely nervous and unsure about myself. The content is still valuable, and that is what matters. Since my first recordings, I've grown more comfortable and confident behind the microphone.

I made sure all the links to specific episodes are free and instantly available to everyone who is reading this. It's my hope that you get a chance to listen to as many as you can, but if you're not near a computer or don't have a live internet connection handy, you can still get all the valuable information the old-fashioned way, by reading it.

SECTION TWO: COURT EMBARRASSMENT

I want you to understand I wasn't always this well informed. That's far from the truth.

I clearly remember a time when I was struggling to be an effective courtroom litigator. And here's the thing: I learned a valuable lesson. Being busy didn't make me better. That doesn't sound logical, but it was my truth. You can't argue with the fact that more litigation experience makes you a better litigator. That's obvious.

But when I was "busy" with a high caseload, I was dealing with many clients, and a high volume practice. I wasn't growing as a litigator. My skills were not advancing. I was plateauing. I was stale and stagnant.

Why? Because I got bogged down with time-consuming business of running the practice. I wasn't experiencing the kinds of things that lead me to being a better lawyer. Instead I was busy tending to…

- Meaningless court status appearances
- Jail visits
- Office hours
- Intake appointments
- Client hand-holding

…all the things in your day that suck the valuable energy and time right out of you. I had nothing left. I didn't have it in me to work on the things that actually make you better.

FIRST D'OH MOMENT

I remember this one time when I got into private practice. I remember walking into court like I owned the place. I was confident. I thought I had a winner on my hands. It was a DWLR. At that time, there were these cases holding that a driver couldn't be revoked multiple times. The details don't matter.

The point is that I went in there, and I asked for a dismissal. I thought my client was entitled to it, and I believed the law was on my side. The prosecutor, without missing a beat, quickly let me know that my case was overruled the week before and that there would be no dismissals on these charges. D'Oh!

What do you think I was telling the client? Just like that, in an instant all my years as a criminal litigator were completely nullified against this young, newly licensed prosecuting attorney who (at that time) knew more than me. But that's how this business of ours works. You know how they love telling us that a criminal courtroom is an adversarial place. That's just your warning that the other side is always trying to destroy your case. In this kind of hostile environment, the attorney who knows the most, has a litigation advantage. As an attorney, you get paid for your brain power and your collective courtroom experience.

Therefore, your ability to learn faster and outthink the other side is your competitive advantage. Outthinking and outperforming the competition in turn ties to how much you know and how quickly you can access all that information in your head. See where I'm going with this?

As a criminal law litigator, what's inside your head matters. That's the mission. To fill it with all the most relevant knowledge, information, and experience you can while maintaining the ability to access it.

SECOND D'OUGH MOMENT

Here's another quick example. This time, I was just sitting around in court, wasting time minding my own business, waiting for another attorney's sentencing hearing to get wrapped up. Counsel was putting on quite a show in his hearing. He called character witnesses, had a full diagnostic report, and mitigation up the wazoo all laid out right there before the judge.

He made his last pitch for probation for his client. The punch line came at the end of the prosecutor's arguments when the prosecutor informed the court that the defendant had been convicted of a non-probationable offense. D'Oh, again! That one hurt. You could see it. It was truly a cringe-worthy moment.

The other attorneys in the room all experienced and felt this moment. Every single attorney knew how it felt to be embarrassingly wrong, ignorant, and horribly misinformed on the law.

But here's the rub, here's the dirty little secret of our profession: there's too much to keep up with. Too many new laws. Too many amendments. Too many reversals. Too many changes and cases to stay on top of. Any attorney who takes their role as counselor seriously understands that there is too much information about the law to read and absorb.

And it's not your fault. Let me say that again, because that's an important point here. It's not your fault. The system is set up this way.

SECTION THREE: WHY PODCASTS WORK

DESIGNED TO FAIL

Let's just assume, for the sake of argument, that you have managed to read through all the most relevant Illinois criminal law treatises. You're reading all the cases, and you devour the most influential case digests and legal updates.

Let's say you're an IllinoisCourts.gov junkie. Let's imagine you're reading all the cases. Let's pretend you've done it. You've figured it out. The management of your practice, your family life, and your skills training is all under control. If you can do all this, then you are truly ahead in the game. You've done it. A podcast may not really help you...unless you want to buy back some of the time you're investing to do all this.

For the rest of us, an audio podcast produced exclusively for Illinois criminal law attorneys can definitely serve the community.

Did you know there are between 20 to 50 published opinions pertaining to Illinois state criminal law released by the Illinois court system? These are precedent carrying cases, not Rule 23 cases. That's 20 to 50 changes, modifications, amendments, or outright reversals of the current law. That's 20 to 50 new ideas, concepts, and new rules you have to hunt down and digest.

The current system is designed for you to fail. The legal landscape changes so fast that any attorney with an active practice and any kind of a home life cannot keep up. It's impossible. Busy attorneys don't have the time or the energy to stay on top of their skill training.

It's that simple. And here's the crux of my thesis. It's not complicated. I'm not trying to be controversial. Those attorneys who manage to find the proper balance in life, practice and not ignoring or shortchanging their litigation skills are the attorneys who will have a competitive advantage.

If you learn how to efficiently keep up and continue to feed your skill base you become the one who is developing the more advanced litigation skills. You're the one in control of your profits and your professional advancement.

I do have good news though. I'm here to say that things have changed. If you are open to what I'm about to say, if you can momentarily suspend all your skepticism and your cynicism, keep an open mind, you'll see why an audio podcast for lawyers is a great idea and you'll see why it works.

The podcast I created is called the Premium Nuggets Podcast. It's an audio-only podcast produced exclusively for Illinois criminal law attorneys. It works the same way any other podcast works. It's not anything incredibly expensive.

It's not some advanced AI system. Absolutely no invasive surgery is required. No computer chips need to be surgically implanted in your head in order for you to transfer the knowledge into your brain.

The Premium Nuggets Podcast draws its content mainly from the changing case law but also covers the new and amended statutes and relevant litigation trends. These are very good reasons why I think this podcast can revolutionize the way Illinois criminal law litigators practice and learn their trade.

In any system with frequently changing rules and norms, it's all about how quickly and easily the updates can be disseminated. Here, any knowledge transfer that can be done without extensive reading has the potential for making the greatest impact.

FLIP THE CASES

So check this out. I'm going to pull some ideas from modern educators. Modern educators like to say that modern technology in the form of online learning has allowed them to "flip the classroom." That's the biggest advantage that they say the modern internet has provided. It's flipped the courtroom.

Well, what the heck does that mean? What they mean by that is that students can now consume education materials at home via YouTube, podcasts, and websites before they even get to school. The time at school is now available for more active learning.

Active learning is the opposite of passive learning. The brain works best when it is creating and processing information, not just consuming it. Thus, active learning is where the rubber hits the road. That's when you ask questions about what you are learning. That's when you get to think critically about the information you are processing. Without an effort to reconcile what you are hearing with what you already know to be true, understanding and learning does not happen. Active listening means listening while analyzing, comparing, and categorizing what you're listening to.

True learning is not a spectator sport. Before online videos and podcasts came along, teachers needed to use valuable classroom time to present the basic material being studied. The lectures and lesson plans provided the raw foundation for learning. Traditionally, a teacher assigned homework which allowed the student the chance to be more active with their learning. But this had to happen at home. The more active and meaningful learning had to happen without supervision. Today, a teacher can "flip" this arrangement.

In a "flipped" classroom a student consumes the foundational elements of a lesson at home via an online video or podcast and now uses the classroom time with the teacher and classmates for more active learning. Teachers much prefer to use the classroom time for active learning activities where guidance and supervision can have a bigger impact.

Similarly, if a podcast produced for Illinois attorneys concentrated on the case law it would effectively "flip" the cases and "flip" the legal learning. Rather than having to spend time and valuable brainpower going through the mechanical process of reading the cases, finding them, sifting through them, all that hard work is already done for you. The bare bones lessons, the nuggets, and the principles available in the case law are extracted and relayed to you automatically with minimal effort on your part at a fraction of the time and energy you would have spent had you hunted down the same facts yourself.

The Premium Nuggets Podcast works the same way. Audio information is transformed into an mp3 file that is heard through an app on your phone and automatically delivered on a regular schedule. This way you listen to the nuggets rather than read them. When you listen you are doing so with a fresh legal mind. And because you have a fresh mind, it means you can listen actively.

You're not wasting valuable brainpower just trying to read, sift, and hunt down the information in the first place. You begin beyond that point. Now you're listening with an active brain that's asking questions, being critical, comparing scenarios, identifying fact patterns, and categorizing the knowledge. But not just any knowledge. We're talking about valuable Illinois courtroom skills and relevant legal updates. This information makes you better in court, warns you of what to look out for. It helps you spot the issues and prevents you from getting side swiped by a big issue on the day of trial.

This is how litigation experience is created, how legal memory is improved, and how you begin to overpower the opposition. Sure, you can still read the cases but an audio podcast multiplies your results. The secret here is that you aren't wasting valuable time and energy reading. The reading is draining your mental resources. You know what I mean if you've ever gotten home from a hard day in court and taken a look at a dense legal document. It hurts just looking at the thing.

With a podcast for the criminal law attorney, audio files are automatically sent to your phone. You learn faster and more efficiently. Remember, outthinking and outperforming the other side is directly tied to how fast you can learn and process legal information. The faster you manage to "flip" your legal learning by "flipping the cases," the larger the explosion in your litigation skills you'll see. This is when you start to develop a permanent litigation advantage over the competition.

HOW THE BRAIN WORKS

I don't want to create an impression that it's all roses and daisies with a podcast. There is also a realistic danger of information overload here.

The problem with making it easy to pump information into your brain is that there is a real risk of overdoing it. Attorneys struggling to make sense of a large volume of information may not be able to access what they need when they need it. The advantage goes to the attorney with the system that allows him or her to access the information at the right time.

So this podcast for Illinois criminal law attorneys has to be produced in such a way that it promotes retention and recall. Without that, we don't have a system. Without that, it's just another time-suck in your day.

Luckily, modern researchers in neurology, psychology, and education know a lot about how the brain works. They know how the brain retains and recalls valuable information.

There's nothing new here, but scientifically there are very good reasons why an audio podcast can lead to an immediate advantage and can streamline your legal learning. It has to be done right. You see, learning, memory, and cognitive studies have established that you remember what you understand. Said differently, that which you can understand will be remembered.

For example, take a simple memory task. If you try to memorize a series of nonsensical words you'll find it almost impossible. Yet, as soon as you can construct a sentence or short story that utilizes the words, you magically remember the words. Experts have known for centuries that people with the best memory are the ones who can couple random bits of information with imagined but familiar mental structures.

These "mental structures" often take the form of, for example, an abstract room in an imaginary castle, parts of your body, or days on a calendar. In the law, we also have pre-established mental structures that form our memory and learning building blocks.

In psychology and cognitive science they call these mental structures schemas. Schemas are just the broad categories used by your brain to organize information. Take, for instance, a criminal trial. You know how the basic steps of a trial work. You know how a trial unfolds, that certain things happen before other things. There are countless law-related schemas used by your brain to make sense of all your new legal concepts and experiences.

There's also a sophisticated filtration system at work here.

This is where information overload can leave you spinning your wheels. Every minute of every day, your brain is exposed to information. I don't just mean the law related information. I mean all of it. The sheer amount of sensory data coming in on a continuous basis can easily overwhelm any processing center, biological or man made.

This stream of data includes everything you see, hear, taste, smell, and touch along with all of your impressions about what you sensed and perceived. It's impossible for your brain to actively process, categorize, and store all this data. Instead, your brain employs a powerful filtration system that determines what will and won't be remembered.

Your legal learning occurs within the confines of this very system. And a podcast for lawyers, to be effective, can take advantage of it. You see, the human memory filter is tied to three key facets of learning. Experts know that:

- Experience
- Emotions and
- Entertainment

can all promote retention and learning. In your brain, in regards to your prior experience and the perception of experience, there are some cool things going on.

You likely already bring a ton of courtroom experience to the table. Immediately then, the information in the podcast makes it past an initial hurdle simply because of the subject matter. To your brain, a podcast about the Illinois criminal law is highly relevant and will pass the initial gatekeeping function.

In the context of the schema theory, your brain already has the filing cabinets built and constructed for the new information you'll be listening to and processing. Your brain is naturally drawn to the subject matter. There is a natural multiplying factor built in here. The more you know the more you can know. The more you listen, the easier it is to retain.

Indeed, schema theory has strong implications for improving your criminal law memory. The more you know about the law, the easier it becomes to learn even more. Learning begets further learning. The more you listen to the podcast the faster you progress. This is because new learning always attaches itself to previously learned material. As the brain builds up folders of information and begins to sort them into the appropriate drawers, your recall and retention of the material naturally improve. New legal concepts and ideas become just a subset or a twist to something you already know, making it that much easier to process and retain.

Coincidentally, we can also look close to home at the work done by researchers in the area of eyewitness identifications. One of the main findings made by these researchers is that memories are created each and every time we ask the brain for a recall. They found that under specific conditions a person was extremely likely to believe a false memory. But what's a false memory?

A false memory is just the translation of raw information into a perceived experience. That is to say that data can quite easily be translated into an experience that is felt, lived, and perceived just like any other real life experience. For audio law learners that means an "audio experience" can be felt in the same manner as any other real life courtroom experience is felt or experienced even though you never actually litigated the case being described. That's crazy! But it's true.

By listening, experience begets more experience. Do you hear what I'm saying? In a very real sense, legal learners are able to gain practical litigation experience simply by listening to the data!

But there's even more going on here. A podcast for Illinois criminal law lawyers has to take into account emotion if it's going to be effective.

It all began with the early history of the human race. Yeah, yeah, I know. I'm not going to spend a lot of time back there. Events from a different millennium had huge effects on how your own brain developed. You see, things that needed to be learned thoroughly were often linked to moments of high emotion. A hunter in imminent danger of death because of a mistake would either perish or survive.

Those who survived would probably perish on a future hunt unless they could remember their mistake well enough to avoid it in the future. What was the difference between those who could remember and those who could not? Well, some had brains that became more active at times of high emotion. The course of evolution favored the survival of people whose memory didn't filter out information that was linked to extreme emotions such as fear, anger, and jealousy.

More recent research has shown that other strong positive emotions like exhilaration can also cause your memory filters to activate. Information that is perceived during emotional times is more likely to be retained. The implications for case law learning is clear. In order to better absorb the information more thoroughly, the material in a podcast should be presented in such a way as to tug on the listener's emotions. Luckily, the case law allows itself to be presented with emotional overtones.

There are always stories embedded in the cases. These stories always have an emotional element. After all, these cases are about a crime. There is almost always a strong emotional element associated with what happened.

Also, the lawyers in a case make decisions that can be examined from an emotional perspective. The lawyers are not above having feelings when they find themselves involved in an intense litigation experience. There's nothing wrong with emphasizing the feelings of the lawyers in a case. The point is that the stories in the cases make it extremely easy to link the material to some emotional element.

Combine this emotional element with your current legal schemas, and you can begin to appreciate how an audio podcast zipping through the case law can begin to explode your own litigation skills. This is exactly how your legal learning and your legal memory can explode.

Finally, any classroom teacher at any level can tell you that a little entertainment value in a presentation goes a long way towards aiding retention. Just ask yourself who were your favorite most impactful teachers? Weren't they the ones who knew how to have a little fun? Super Bowl advertisers know how to get football fans to remember their products. Modern news programs understand that a little entertainment goes a long way towards capturing attention.

The entire movie industry lives off making movies as entertaining as possible. The best directors are the ones that know how to turn this glamour and glitz into memorable informative commentaries. My point is that although a podcast for lawyers doesn't need to break down into slapstick or stand-up comedy, when it's appropriate, a little fun and humor doesn't hurt anything.

In fact, a little entertainment actually enhances your legal learning. Once you understand what's going on in your head, you can begin to appreciate how an audio podcast designed specifically for Illinois criminal law practitioners can be effectively and efficiently utilized. When you understand how it all works you can begin to imagine how you can use a podcast to transform your own practice. I think you can now begin to see why I'm so excited about this idea and why I think an audio podcast is a valuable resource for you and our colleagues.

AUDIO LEARNING FOR LAWYERS

As you've probably already guessed, this podcast already exists and it has a name. I've been describing the Premium Nuggets Podcast.

Surprise. Surprise. This is the only podcast produced exclusively for Illinois criminal law attorneys. This is the only podcast that actively utilizes all the mental systems I have described to help make attorneys top notch litigators in their field.

The Premium Nuggets Podcast aims to get all the most relevant and useful nuggets of information in the current cases off the paper and into your head. With the Premium

Nuggets, you hear about the cases rather than read them. The important details "stick" in that noggin of yours because the information gets assimilated and processed alongside related information.

Up until now, a lawyer had to read the cases and apply what they learned in the courtroom or trial setting. And let me be clear, actual courtroom experience and in depth legal research on specific legal issue is never going away. Boiled down to its core, the Premium Nuggets Podcast is a supplement to your general legal education efforts, a supplement with an explosive punch.

It's a legal learning tool that promises to work efficiently by effectively multiplying your applied litigation skills. The Premium Nuggets Podcast is, simply stated, the easiest, most effective form of technology that allows you to manage your courtroom skills training.

SECTION FOUR: DUI ROADBLOCKS

When I started looking around for criminal law subjects to podcast about, I thought that the topic of roadblocks and DUI checkpoints was a great place to start.

There really wasn't anything new happening in that area, but I always liked how basic knowledge with just a few cases was all an attorney needed to know to master that area. Really, though, this is true for every issue an Illinois criminal law lawyer is likely to confront in court.

So this is a great area of the law that really illustrates the great partnership between a niche podcast, a great lawyer, and a relevant legal topic. We begin with dissecting the law on DUI checkpoints (also called roadblocks).

I originally recorded the material on this topic in podcast episode 036.

You can listen to it for free by plugging the url below into your nearest browser:

https://IllinoisCaseLaw.com/036

I want to begin with the general law in this area. I'll provide a general overview then I'll get into three general cases that provide the foundation in this area.

I used to be a teacher, and I'm still a lawyer. There is always going to be a part of me that wants to teach this stuff as opposed to just regurgitate the material repeating the black and white letter law. In this very specific case it's very important to have this general foundation of the law under your belt. You're going to see that when we get to the second part, when we start answering questions, if we understand the fundamentals a lot of the questions will essentially answer themselves.

DUI ROADBLOCK FOUNDATION

People v. Ray, 327 Ill. App. 3d 904 (5th 2002) is the first case we'll look at. Because I practice in Illinois, I'm a little more familiar with these cases. But *People v. Ray* is important because it depends on an Illinois Supreme Court case. That case is really the important case in this area. That case is *City of Indianapolis v. Edmond*, 531 U.S. 32, 121 S.Ct. 447 (2000).

The *Edmond* case stands for the general principle that any generalized checkpoint or roadblock is illegal. So what's a generalized checkpoint? Well, in *People v. Ray* the state troopers set up a roadblock. They were running a general drug interdiction, which just means they were looking for drugs in cars driving on the roadway.

It was not a DUI checkpoint, nor was it done for a specific investigation. They just wanted to stop cars to search for drugs. It was an organized roadblock. They had the signs out directing drivers into specific lanes. All the officers had traffic control vests. The police had an organized briefing before they got started where they dolled out responsibilities and assignments for the participating officers. They had the drug dogs out there conducting roadside sniffings.

Most of the questions they had for drivers revolved around drugs. You know stuff like: Where are you coming from? Is there anything illegal in the car? Where are the drugs? Who's sniffing that nose candy today? That kind of stuff.

One individual in this case was arrested for drug possession. He challenges the traffic stop in court by arguing that this type of a roadblock is unconstitutional. He said general drug interdiction checkpoints like this one are strictly illegal. *City of Indianapolis v. Edmond* is the foundation case for this principle.

Defendant Ray was correct. The court said this type of safety checkpoint or roadblock set up for general crime control is illegal. You cannot set up a roadblock just to search for crime in general. It's illegal, unconstitutional, can't be done, and it won't be allowed.

One interesting side note about *People v. Ray* was that the police did put up signs advertising that there was going to be a roadblock set up. But they provided inaccurate information about exactly where it would be. They said it would be at one place and they actually set it up somewhere else. They were stopping the cars that tried to avoid the checkpoint. Those cars were sure to get extra attention from the police. So, general crime control investigations are out.

ILLINOIS V. LIDSTER

Then we get a case called *Illinois v. Lidster*, 540 U.S. 419, 124 S.Ct. 885 (2004). This one came out of the Illinois court system. It made its way to the Illinois Supreme Court and then went to the Supreme Court of the United States.

The facts in this case are a little bit different. There was a roadblock. But the court said that in this case this roadblock was not a generalized crime control roadblock. Instead, it was an information-seeking type of stop or checkpoint. You see, the rest of the facts in *Lidster* are that the day before, and it's important that something happened just the day before, there was a hit and run that resulted in the death of a pedestrian.

They had a homicide. A driver hit a person, killed him, and then drove away. The police were thinking that if they could set up a roadblock in and around the area of where this hit and run occurred and at about the time of day that it happened, they may be able to find other drivers who saw something. They figured most drivers probably drive near the same area at the same time of day as they go to and from work or wherever. So they thought they had a decent chance of finding some witnesses. It was not an illogical conclusion to draw.

The court said this was legal. This roadblock was allowed. What's the main difference between *Lidster* and *Ray*? Both cases involved criminal investigations. But the target of the investigation in *Lidster* were not the individual drivers being questioned by the police. The drivers in the *Lidster* case were seen and treated as witnesses to a crime. In the best case scenario, the police were hoping for information about what they may have seen in and around that area the day before. Stuff like, "yeah I did see a car suddenly stop. The driver got out and then sped away." But the drivers were not under investigation themselves. They didn't really expect to arrest the drivers or even expect to find the person who hit the pedestrian.

The court said because the focus of the investigation was not the driver but instead was a different person it was not considered a generalized form of crime control and that roadblock was considered legal.

What's important to know about these cases is that the court is always going to conduct a balancing test in answering these questions. A balancing test was also run in *People v. Ray*, but the answer just came out differently. What do I mean by a balancing test? I just mean that the judges are going to sit there and weigh or balance the competing interests in the cases. They are asking themselves:

"Is the gravity of the public concern for public safety in this hit and run investigation bigger than than the severity of the interference of individual driver's rights?"

Said differently you can think of it this way:

> "Is stopping these cars to ask for information about a homicide more important than momentarily stopping individuals who are on their way home from work?"

In *Lidster,* the court said, and I'm paraphrasing here, that

> "Yeah, it is more important to let the officers proceed with their investigation than to worry about interfering with the ride home most drivers were undertaking."

It's basically that simple. The court took many factors into account in reaching this conclusion and conducting this balancing test.

For example, they emphasized that this was all about progressing a murder investigation. That's significant. That's an enormous state interest. But from the driver's perspective the concerns are minimized. They figured that once a driver saw what was going on, and they realized they were not under investigation themselves, they would probably agree the police were doing a really good thing. The judges felt the driver's guard would come down. They would feel less anxiety and less stress about being stopped in the first place. It was even possible the drivers would feel good about being able to help as opposed to feeling the dread and discomfort that comes when knowing you have been made the target of a police investigation. So that's basically the gist. There's always a balancing of interests.

If you go back and look at *People v. Ray* through this balancing act regime, you at first may think that there is also an important state interest involved in that case. Who doesn't want to get drugs off the streets? Isn't cleaning up drugs off our streets more important than momentarily stopping an individual? Seems logical.

The problem is that things look very different from the driver's perspective. Now the burden and the stress of the police interaction is much different. The anxiety for the driver skyrockets because the driver soon realizes they are under investigation.

If you get pulled over in what appears to be a random way and are suddenly asked where you keep your drugs and where you're coming from the situation is now completely different. Now you are not being asked to aid and assist. Now you're the target and you instantly become more defensive. Now the balancing test is skewed the other way and the courts say "no" to that type of general crime control when individual drivers are the target. Suddenly, it's easier for a court to say the whole thing is unreasonable and therefore impermissible.

PEOPLE V. BARTLEY

So you can kind of see where the courts are coming from. This gets us into the DUI situation. *People v. Bartley*, 109 Ill. 2d 273, 486 N.E.2d 880 (1985), is the next case here. Again, this is an Illinois Supreme Court case.

I'm extremely confident every other state has an analogous decision saying the same thing said in *Bartley* and coming to the same conclusions and findings. This is the Illinois

Supreme Court case that said that DUI checkpoints in this state are legal and proper.

They are constitutional and reasonable. The same balancing act discussed earlier is still being conducted here. Right now, a lot of people may be thinking that this does not make sense. How can this be legal? I don't understand. The fourth amendment says that people can't be stopped for any reason. A DUI checkpoint is randomly stopping cars. What gives? If they don't have any reason to believe that I am driving drunk how can they legally stop me?

So let's break it down. First thing to remember is exactly what the Constitution says. The Constitution actually says an individual has the right to be secure "against unreasonable searches and seizures." U. S. Const. amend. IV. Period. That's the exact language in the United States Constitution. It doesn't say that you can never be searched or stopped without probable cause. The actual language is just that you have a right to be secure against unreasonable searches and seizures. Everything else is invented by judges in the courts. It will be these same courts that are answering questions about DUI checkpoints and their legality.

Courts don't necessarily begin with asking about probable cause and reasonable suspicion. They begin with asking if these stops are reasonable. That's the basic question for them. And that's where these balancing tests really ultimately come from. The balancing act does not come from what you see on TV but instead comes from those words in the Constitution. The basic question that they are answering is whether a DUI roadblock or safety checkpoint is reasonable. This is the ultimate question in these cases. To answer that question they developed the balancing test.

It is reasonable if the state interest in DUI deterrence and stopping roadside deaths is bigger than the interest in privacy against being stopped. And so there it is.

People v. Bartley conducted this balancing and came out in favor of allowing this type of roadblock. The case discussed the balance between public safety and the degree of intrusion into an individual's privacy.

In the analysis, they don't spend a lot of time describing the state interest. They devote two lines of text to mention the state interest and that's because it's usually pretty clear. In this case the state interest is in stopping people from being killed on our roadways. That's not something most people are going to argue with. They state the interest as fact and then they move on. Where they spend most of their time is with the private interests.

And what is the private interest? The private interest is in getting home and not being stopped or harassed by the police. For that, the courts are really looking at two types of factors. They are looking at what they call objective factors, and they are looking at some subjective factors. The objective factors are just the objective manifestations of the stop which describe what the physical aspects of the stop look like. Where are the roadblocks being set up? How was it conducted? How long does it take? How are the officer's dressed? Are there visible signs and clear directions? That sort of thing.

When they consider the objective factors on the private interest, they conclude that the interference is pretty small.

The courts point out that the actual interaction with police during one of these safety check type roadblocks is pretty brief. The duration of the stop is measured in seconds, certainly less then a minute. The courts say an average stop takes between 15 and 20 seconds, and they note that to be a minimal obstruction. They are usually done in a highly visible area. Often there is clear signage at the scene. The roadblocks are advertised and publicized heavily. A driver's physical safety is rarely endangered. Objectively, no driver is being put in physical danger, and the whole thing takes a minimal amount of time. This makes the objective factors pretty minimal.

Where the court spends a lot of time is in the analysis of the subjective factors. The analysis looks at the experience of the drivers. The subjective experiences from the citizen's perspective is the focus. Subjectively, what is the driver experiencing during the roadside roadblock experience? They look at all the factors that can have an effect on the subjective experience of the driver.

For example, they looked at the perception of the driver. They ask if the driver would have been aware of the procedural guidelines being used to conduct the roadblock. Drivers experience less anxiety if they perceive that there are rules being followed, that this is not just a renegade cop, a renegade police station doing god knows what. The more this feels like an official operation that has procedural guidelines the less taxing it will be. They're looking for the absence of discretion. It's the perception that officers are not picking on cars in a random *ad hoc* manner. Drivers want to know that the officers that are talking to them are following rules and that they didn't get picked randomly. This means the more apparent that it is that the police don't have the discretion to stop who they want the less stressful it will be. We want to know that it's an official operation. We want to know that it's supervised. And we want to know that rules are being followed.

In order to know that the whole thing is being supervised, it's helpful to see supervisors on the scene supervising. We want to see higher ranking officers that can be easily identified. We want to see them answering questions and doing their thing. The selection of the site by the supervisor is just as important. We want to know that the driver understands that this is going to be a very minimal experience. If drivers see that they will get in and get out in a hurry and be on their way quickly the whole thing doesn't seem so bad. All of it, the whole kit and kaboodle, needs to send the message to the driver that "I'm not being harassed."

When we go back and we look at *People v. Bartley*, what the court said was that not each and every single type of roadblock is going to be the same. Sometimes the factors considered will lead to a finding that a roadblock was illegal, other times a roadblock may be found to be perfectly legal. If a roadblock is set up in such a way that the subjective perceptions of the driver are worse, this could affect the overall balancing. If a roadblock looks good on paper but is executed poorly this could tip the scales into illegal stops. Under all these varying scenarios the exact same state interest is always at play.

As a general principle, if a roadside safety check roadblock is set up "correctly" it will be considered legal. A "correct" roadblock is one that minimizes the subjective anxiety experienced by the driver. So, "correct" ones will have clear plans and procedures, a written policy, it will be highly publicized, properly supervised, and it will have clear signage so everyone knows what they have to do and officers will have restricted discretion when they are on the scene.

The person in the car may not see any actual written policies or rules. That stuff is usually what the lawyers fight about and litigate in court, but that's the general idea. In principle, the courts are going to allow a DUI checkpoint, but if one is conducted improperly or incorrectly it could be attacked in court, DUI arrests could be dismissed, and charges dropped.

I know I spent a good chunk of time on these preliminary issues but the more you understand the root principles the easier everything else will fall into place. Simply by having some basic knowledge and awareness of these three cases you can answer just about every other important question that could pop up around roadblocks. This is true even if the information in the question doesn't appear to be covered by the facts in these cases. By knowing the basics and the fundamentals, a knowledgeable person or attorney can deduce reasonably correct answers.

ANSWER THE TOP 10 QUESTIONS

So let's take a look at some of these questions. For example, a common question that an attorney may get from a client about DUI checkpoints is:

(1) **"Do I even have to cooperate?"** The easy answer is "yes." If they are asking, *"Do I have to stop?"* then, "yes," of

course they do. At a minimum level, a person has to stop at the roadblocks. You can't run over barricades and crash through squad cars.

When we say the stop at a roadblock is legal we inherently mean that drivers have to legally stop and present their driver's license, insurance, and registration. An officer has a right to check all those things in every traffic stop. So a driver would be obliged to comply with those demands. So if a person was wondering if he or she had to give his or her driver's license, the answer is "yes." Beyond that, a driver probably doesn't have to do much else.

(2) **"Ok, but do I have to roll down my window?"** You don't have to cooperate in any other way. For example, answering other questions and rolling down the window are probably not required. But you still have to stop and roll down your window enough to give up your license.

Obviously, I'm only talking about the legal aspects of police DUI roadblocks. I'm not giving suggestions or ideas on how a person should conduct themselves at these things. This is not legal advice on what a driver should do or not do. Also, this is just how one attorney is thinking about these ideas. This does not mean that the police you face at your next checkpoint feel the same way. They may share some of these ideas and may completely disregard them as well.

(3) **"Can I avoid the roadblock by turning around or going another way?"** Well, I would say that you should be able to drive away or turn away without problems. There is nothing inherently suspicious about avoiding a roadblock. Sure, a criminal with guns and drugs in the car would likely want to avoid the roadblock, but so would any innocent

driver who wants to get home hassle-free and in a hurry. The only exception here would be that a driver can't break the law or violate other traffic ordinances in their attempt to avoid a roadblock. If you perform a risky lane violation or do anything else that puts other drivers or the police in harm's way, the cops could stop you for those reasons. If you draw their attention in any other way, they may want to see what your big hurry is all about.

But if you can do it cleanly, avoiding a roadblock is not illegal. You can't get in trouble for it, and officers can't legally stop you just because you turned around to avoid the roadblock. But the Illinois Supreme Court has made it clear that they feel differently. In March of 2016 they released the case of *People v. Timmsen*, 2016 IL 118181 (March). You can listen to the summary here:

https://IllinoisCaseLaw.com/153

In that case, a driver was seen performing a U-turn to avoid a DUI roadblock. Police see this and they send an officer in a squad to pull over the defendant. The driver is not drunk but is driving on a suspended license and has some cannabis on him, so he gets arrested. Defendant challenged his stop, arguing that the U-turn was not illegal and that there was nothing suspicious about avoiding the checkpoint.

The Illinois high court came in to say that the U-turn itself could create a reasonable suspicion of wrongdoing solely because it was done to avoid contact with the police at the roadblock. The high court said that anytime an individual is seen trying to avoid contact with the police it's reasonable for the police to believe that this is suspicious. The court said that citizens do have a right to go about their business avoiding police if they want, but this defendant was not just going on about his way. The U-turn was an act purposely designed to avoid the police. It explicitly meant a change from the driver's course of travel. It was clear he was trying to avoid the traffic checkpoint, and that is suspicious. The court did say there is no bright-line rule saying you can get stopped anytime you avoid a roadblock. Every case has to be evaluated on its own facts. However, because this driver was taking evasive action, it rose to the level of suspicious activity.

Timmsen is a great example of how the fundamental cases help set us up and help us make arguments one way or another. Ultimately, the high court in any jurisdiction gets the final say on specific issues. It's up to us to keep up with the issues and be aware of the nuance being flushed out by the courts.

(4) **"Can the police put up fake signs where they misidentify the location of the roadblock?"** Can they say the roadblock is at exit B but they really set it up at exit A hoping to catch everyone trying to avoid the thing? Police can't do this.

If you think about it from the subjective perspective of the drivers, the problem with this becomes apparent. Public awareness and publicity of the roadblocks are factors that weigh in favor of a reasonable roadblock. When the public is aware of the roadblock it feels more like a professional operation and doesn't feel like a random chaotic operation. The point of the roadblock is not to make DUI arrests.

The interest of the police and the state is to save lives and prevent fatal car accidents. That's how it was argued in court. They are not there to round up drunk drivers, make arrests, and increase finds. They are there to discourage the drunk driver from driving in the first place. The more that the public is aware of the roadblocks the more the word gets out about them and the less likely there will be drunk driving.

People will lineup their designated drivers, order their Uber cars, and do what they have to do to make it through the checkpoints safe and sound. That's the point of the whole thing. If fake signs or misleading advertising gets out, that will destroy the public's positive will and attitude towards the thing. A public safety operation would instantly feel like a criminal investigation targeting the drivers.

So fake signage counteracts the state interest and heightens the perceived anxiety subjectively experienced by the public. Fake signs could tip the balance towards a finding of an unreasonable DUI roadblock. No fake signs, no trickery, everything has to be legitimate.

(5) **"Do I have to answer the questions being asked by the officers during the DUI roadblock?"** You can kind of guess the types of questions officers may typically ask during the stop. How's your evening? Where you coming from? Where you going? Have you been drinking tonight? Interestingly, the questions and answers often don't really matter. The police just want to make visual contact with the drivers. They want to see the driver's face, eyes, and general appearance. If there are any distinct odors coming from the car the police want to be aware of that.

So technically, you don't have to answer their questions. There is no legal penalty for refusing to answer. I guess there are two ways to not answer. You can say, "I'm not going to answer any questions officer I just want to be on my way." Or you can just sit there mute pretending like you can't hear them actively choosing to not answer. Remember, I'm not giving legal advice here on what you should or shouldn't do during a traffic stop. I'm just looking at the legal aspects of these situations.

Theoretically, if the officer doesn't have any other reason to believe that you've had a seizure or become unresponsive because of a stroke or something, they can't hold the decision to go mute against you. They can still make their observations and size you up even though you ain't speaking. The officer may ask, "Sir, have you had anything to drink tonight?" And you say nothing. Long pause. Long pause. "Sir, are you feeling well tonight?" And you say nothing. Long pause. Long pause. They can still look you up and down and size you up. They can still take a peek inside the car. They can still look for empty whisky bottles and beer cans thrown about the back seat.

Whether you answer the questions or not they can still make their observations and assessments and let you move on. If they are not seeing signs of inebriation, or physical illness they have to let you go and move you along. Technically, "no" you don't have to answer their questions. Practically, what will actually happen if you don't? Who knows. That just depends on the officer you draw.

You may be there longer than you otherwise would have been. Maybe you aggravate the officer and that leads to other problems, but in a perfect world there should be no consequence for refusing to answer the officer's questions at a DUI roadblock. If you get lucky and draw an officer who is disciplined, who is reasonable, and who knows the law, and knows the purpose of the checkpoint you'll be alright. If you get unlucky and draw a cowboy with a short fuse than anything can happen.

(6) **"Can they pull me out of the car?"** Generally, no, but there is always a caveat. Ordinarily, the general scope of the stop does not include getting out of your car. But if there is something about your demeanor, your answers to the questions, or if anything else happens that creates suspicion that something else is going on, then "yea" the officers can get you out of the car. If they have a reason to get you out, they can. All things being equal, the faster they can get drivers through the experience, the more reasonable it is.

So, taking the time to pull every driver out is on its face unreasonable. Additionally, drivers are exposed to more physical risk, and by that point the subjective fear and anxiety of the drivers is going through the roof. Obviously, if the police officers begin to suspect intoxication that would be a reason to get you out for more observation including field sobriety tests.

(7) **"Will I have to do field sobriety tests?"** This question is very similar to the previous one, and the answer is also similar. It is a DUI safety checkpoint afterall. But "no." The vast majority of drivers spend around 15 seconds during the whole thing. So that doesn't leave time for field sobriety tests. The detention is brief in scope, limited in nature, and limited

to observations and odors. The stop is all about what the officer can see and smell in 15 seconds.

As soon as the police think they see something that creates a red flag, then they can ask you to drive into a different inspection lane where the real fun begins. At that point, if they have reason to suspect, then they can have you perform the field sobriety tests.

Generally, you won't be asked to do field sobriety tests unless the officer sees signs of intoxication like slurred speech, the odor of drinking, and red, itchy eyes. Interestingly, police having any reason to believe you have consumed any amount of alcohol could provoke the field sobriety tests. They don't have to be certain you are drunk or that you drank a lot, but signs of drinking in any amount could justify further inquiry.

So, answering the question, "have you had anything to drink tonight?" with the answer "just one officer" could justify the field sobriety tests. It doesn't mean it will happen, but at that point, the police have the right to investigate further.

(8) **"Will I have to blow?"** Probably not. All the same principles in the previous two questions and answers are at play here as well. Usually, a portable breathalyzer sample is not asked for until after field sobriety tests have been performed.

So if this happens, it won't happen until they are well underway in suspecting a DUI. Why don't they just ask every driver to blow at the beginning and forget the questions? That would take too long and would increase the driver's subjective anxiety about the experience. If a driver gets to a situation where he or she is being asked to blow at a DUI roadblock then that means the police are well on their way into a full DUI investigation.

Refusing to blow at that point would have all the same ramifications as it would during an ordinary DUI investigation. So you can refuse to blow, but if they think they have a legitimate DUI arrest, all the suspended drivers license provisions would kick in. That area of the law is generally called the implied consent laws and that's a rabbit hole we ain't jumping into now.

(9) **"Can they have a drug dog out there?"** *People v. Ray* was a drug interdiction roadblock. They did have dogs at the scene in that case. That roadblock was found to be illegal. But we can't conclude everytime a dog is at a safety checkpoint that the whole thing is now illegal. The dogs can be there. The question is how does the presence of the dog impact the subjective experience of the drivers. The presence of the drug dog can't affect the other factors. The stop can't be delayed so the dog can sniff every car. They can't hold you longer just to get a sniff. The dog certainly can't be used in an aggressive or intimidating manner. All those factors come back on the table when we think about the presence of drug dogs at DUI checkpoints. If a dog does alert to the presence of something then that could provide a basis for further police scrutiny.

(10) **"Can I exercise my constitutional rights at a police roadside safety checkpoint?"** A DUI roadblock may be perceived by some to be a momentary suspension of a driver's constitutional rights. Afterall, we are allowing police to stop cars driven by people who have done nothing wrong.

But, if anything, the point of this analysis is to highlight that police can stop a car at a DUI roadblock precisely because of the Constitution. Constitutional rights are not being suspended or infringed upon. The Constitution is being obeyed and honored. So an individual would be able to exercise any other constitutional rights one has during the roadblock. Cars ain't going through a twilight zone or anything. Any other rights you are aware of and you know how to exercise will be available. You do have to stop, provide your license and registration, and are free to exercise all your other rights.

I like these cases on DUI roadblocks because they illustrate how general awareness of just a few cases can really help explain and illuminate an entire area of the fourth amendment jurisprudence. Any attorney who catches a DUI case from a roadblock will instantly know where to look to see if they have any viable issues in the case. We can form a body of knowledge predicated on a very small amount of information.

When you know the fundamentals you know a lot more than just the facts that are contained in the cases. A person who wants to get this information in their head can do what I did and just hunt down the cases. Read them carefully and note the important principles...or they can listen to the cases and get to the same results much quicker and more efficiently. They can listen, that is, if someone has gone through the trouble to create the audio summary and made the information available to others.

SECTION FIVE: THE MEANING OF PROOF BEYOND A REASONABLE DOUBT

You would have thought that the courts would have a working definition of proof beyond a reasonable doubt. There's probably no more basic or fundamental idea than what we mean when we say a defendant has to be convicted with proof beyond a reasonable doubt.

ILLINOIS IS DIFFERENT

Yet, in 2015 the Illinois Supreme Court had to revisit the definition of proof beyond a reasonable doubt. The court had to confront how best to respond to a jury when they ask for a definition of proof beyond a reasonable doubt. Inevitably, a jury is likely to ask for a definition from the judge and the lawyers on a case. And why shouldn't they ask for one?

Everything else is defined for them with nice little definitions, no matter how basic a concept. We give them working definitions for words like "possession" and "knowingly" and many more. It's actually quite natural for a jury to ask for a working definition of what their burden is.

Basically, they are just asking for clarification on exactly what it is they are being asked to do. Yet, in Illinois, unlike other states and even the federal system, our courts have refused to give a definition to the jury on what we mean when we tell them to convict with proof beyond a reasonable doubt.

We don't do it. Proof beyond a reasonable doubt is a special term in Illinois, and the courts instead leave it up to the jury to ponder the question. When the question or request for a definition comes up, judges and lawyers routinely take a pass. So what's going on?

The basic idea here is that Illinois courts say the term, "proof beyond a reasonable doubt," speaks for itself. Any attempt to use other words or phrases to further explain the concept will just lead to confusion and introduce error into the process. The court system takes the position that the best thing to do is tell the jury they must convict when the state has proved its case with proof beyond a reasonable doubt. Then they leave it up to the jury to wrestle with the meaning. They believe a typical jury has the ability to figure out how to apply that standard in a case. That's what deliberation is all about.

So we don't give them a definition. This creates this confusing and awkward situation in the middle of some jury deliberations when the jury sends a note to the judge asking for a definition of the standard they are to apply. The judges and the lawyers are left with a situation where the jury has to be responded to, yet the attorneys don't really have anything new to tell them. Frequently, in these situations the jury may get a response that simply tells them that they have already been given all the instructions that they need to come to a verdict, and they don't tell them anything new.

Another way the judge and the attorneys handle the question is by simply repeating back what they have already told the jury but in a different way.

The jury could be told that proof beyond a reasonable doubt does not include any doubts that are reasonable. These are the games that are played and the non-answer responses often given to a jury. The jury, no doubt, thought they were asking a serious question and were likely expecting a serious response.

Yet, the attorneys and the judge often know the case law highly disfavors giving the jury any kind of definition that differs from the words and the phrase itself. Throw in the fact that the court has an obligation to answer legal questions for the jury and, I guess, it should be of no surprise that the Illinois Supreme Court had to take a look at this issue.

The definition of "proof beyond a reasonable doubt" is as legal a question as there can be. A court is obligated to answer all the legal questions a jury may ask. Yet, the lawyers were aware that if they came up with a definition different from the phrase itself the appellate court would likely strike down the conviction.

So this was the situation. The jury, the judge and the attorneys are all stuck in this place of open loops and weird responses. I personally have tried to come up with various ways to tell the jury something on this topic. Keep in mind, they had to ask for a definition on their own accord. Most of the time attorneys are just hoping and praying they won't be asked for anything beyond the initial jury instructions.

Most of the ideas I had relied on were some version of a non-answer answer or a circular reasoning answer. Those were things like this:

THE NON-ANSWER ANSWER
"You have all the instructions necessary for you to reach a decision in this case."

CIRCULAR REASONING ANSWER
"Reasonable doubt is simply a doubt that is reasonable. If you have any doubt of defendant's guilt it is for you to determine if that doubt is reasonable."

Well, hopefully you can appreciate the mess we found ourselves in every time a jury wanted to know more about proof beyond a reasonable doubt.

I began by saying that in 2015 the Illinois Supreme Court took a look at this issue. I'm happy to say that, for now, they have clarified the situation a little more for us.

PEOPLE V. DOWNS

We still have to worry about what to say to a jury when they ask for a definition of proof beyond a reasonable doubt. And as far as I can tell, juries will continue to ask this question. So it's quite instructive to dive into the recent history on this issue.

In *People v. Downs*, 2015 IL 117934 (June), the jury sent a note to the judge asking about the meaning of proof beyond a reasonable doubt.

You can listen to the 10-minute episode where I first outlined this case here:

https://IllinoisCaseLaw.com/080

In this case, the exact question they wrote to the judge was:

> *"What is your definition of reasonable doubt?*
> *80%, 70%, or 60%?"*

That was the extent of the question. The judge and the attorneys replied with a note of their own saying something very similar to how most judges and attorneys would have replied. They wrote back:

> *"We cannot give you a definition.*
> *It is your duty to define."*

That was the extent of the reply. Well, this was a murder trial that was reversed by the appellate court. The appellate court said it was reversible error to answer that way because it was clear from the jury's question that they were thinking of "proof beyond a reasonable doubt" as percentages. The appellate court took note of the fact that they went as low as 60%.

To the appellate court it looked like the jury was thinking of something way less than the high standard we all know it to be. It's the highest legal standard recognized in American courts, and, whatever it means, it has to mean something higher than 60%. The appellate court said that under these circumstances, merely telling them that it is their duty to define the burden for themselves was like green lighting a lesser burden for them. In other words, telling the jury that that it was their duty to define the burden was literally telling them to define it how they saw fit, even as something less than 60%.

The Illinois Supreme Court stepped in to reverse the appellate court. This means the high court did not find the response to the jury to constitute reversible error. So the trial court got it right. Sort of.

The Court said that on its face it may seem like the jury was being told they could define the term however they wanted, but there was really no proof of that. The jury still had all the other instructions. Including the one that told them in order to convict they had to find the state proved its case with proof beyond a reasonable doubt.

So there was no reason to believe the jury misunderstood the standard or applied it differently. Factually, it's correct to tell a jury that they must define the term for themselves. That is what has to actually happen, and it's not reversible error to tell them that...if they ask. It is not reversible error to respond in that manner.

The decision in *Downs* had been building up, and it was inevitable that the high court would have to get involved because there were other appellate court decisions saying that telling a jury they must define the term proof beyond a reasonable doubt for themselves was reversible error. Those cases were all overruled by *People v. Downs*.

PEOPLE V. THOMAS

For example, one of these cases was *People v. Thomas*, 2014 IL App (2d) 121203 (August). You can listen to the 11-minute episode summarizing this case by following the link below:

https://IllinoisCaseLaw.com/010

In *Thomas*, the jury was trying to decide if the defendant was guilty of retail theft. The question they asked the court was:

"What is the legal definition of reasonable doubt?"

The answer provided by the court was:

"It is for you to determine."

This time the appellate court didn't reverse. You could see the appellate court was trying to stop a wave of reversals that would result if they struck down that response. Specifically, the court in *Thomas* said that even if it didn't like the response that was given to the jury or if it thought it was the wrong response, it would not reverse without proof that the jury actually applied a lesser standard during their deliberations.

In other words, in order to reverse a conviction the appellate court was going to look for proof that the jury likely applied a lower standard than proof beyond a reasonable doubt.

This set up a situation where the Supreme Court had to get involved because the different appellate courts were treating the issue differently.

There truly was turmoil on this issue among the various appellate courts in Illinois. *Thomas* does a good job of summarizing the important cases on the topic. The case mentions *People v. Turman*, 2011 IL App (1st) 091019 (June). The definition of reasonable doubt given to the jury in that case was:

> *"It is for the jury to collectively determine what reasonable doubt is."*

That court reasoned that the conviction had to be reversed because that statement to the jury allowed the jury to use a standard that, in all likelihood, was below the threshold of a reasonable doubt standard. The court did not explain why this likelihood was so high. Yet, we had two appellate courts with different rulings pertaining to the exact same answer to the jury.

PEOPLE V. FRANKLIN

Then there was *People v. Franklin*, 2012 IL App (3d) 100618 (June). The reasonable doubt definition given to the jury here when they asked for one was:

> *"It's what each of you individually and collectively, as 12 of you, believe is beyond a reasonable doubt."*

That court reversed the conviction for a similar reason.

The reviewing court said that the trial court's instruction created a reasonable likelihood that the jury had convicted the defendant based on a standard of proof less than beyond a reasonable doubt.

Thus, *Franklin* found that anytime a definition for beyond a reasonable doubt other than the words themselves is given, *per se* reversible error occurs. You can see how for a while there attorneys went into a trial hoping to God the jury did not ask for further instructions on what it means to convict with proof beyond a reasonable doubt.

To be clear, the Illinois Supreme Court is now saying it's acceptable to tell a jury, when they ask, that it is up to them to define the term of proof beyond a reasonable doubt for themselves.

Interestingly, *Downs* was a Second Appellate Court Case, and so was *Thomas*. The Illinois Supreme Court reversed the Second District in *Downs* but they essentially applied the exact test and standard that the Second District announced in *Thomas*. Weird, right?

WHAT TO TELL THE JURY

The big takeaway for lawyers is that we want the jury to wrestle with this issue. That's what the job at hand requires. That's what having a jury system is all about. We want them to go back and forth with each other making sense of the standard and how it applies to the facts of the case. We do want them to come up with a working meaning and definition for themselves, so long as we stress that this is the highest burden that the law recognizes, and that whatever working definition they come up with has to be consistent with this idea. Sure, this is hard. It may make juries uncomfortable, but we can't spoon feed them everything. Their job is not easy but important.

Maybe we've just been asking the wrong question all along. Maybe it's not about providing the appropriate definition for reasonable doubt. The real question that matters here is what is the appropriate legal standard to apply in our criminal justice system? If that's the question we are asking, then the answer is that we should be applying the standard of proof beyond a reasonable doubt.

That's where we are at with this issue in Illinois. The court says those simple words speak for themselves, and we don't need to cloud up the issue with more words that supposedly clarify the meaning. What matters is that they are applying the correct legal standard. The answer to that question is proof beyond a reasonable doubt.

Juries are going to keep asking the question, and they are going to want to know what the definition of proof beyond a reasonable doubt is. In my opinion, the best way to answer the question is to throw it back at the jury, but not in the way we've been reading about in these decisions. The best way is probably to tell them that the answer they seek is in the instructions they have already received. It's best to remind them that they have all the instructions required to reach a verdict.

Fun stuff, right?

SECTION SIX: THE KRANKEL TWO-STEP (THE INQUIRY AND THE HEARING)

I'm fond of saying that in the criminal law we peddle in headache and heartache. Nothing good comes out of a criminal prosecution. At the end of the process the possibility that a defendant will remain upset and unsatisfied is practically guaranteed.

Which brings up the interesting topic of how a trial court should handle the complaints of a defendant saying that he is very unsatisfied with his own attorney and complains that his counsel was ineffective.

PEOPLE V. KRANKEL

Private attorneys may tend to ignore this area of the law under the mistaken assumption that this mainly is a public defender problem. Some of these attorneys may think they are "cool" with their clients or that they are providing such diligent service that they'd never get a claim of ineffective assistance from a disgruntled client.

I've learned that it doesn't matter how hard you worked or how much you think you have bonded with a client. When a decision comes down they don't like, which is likely to happen, at that moment you are dead to them. Wise and experienced counsel knows that it's only a matter of time before they are standing before a judge with a client who is ratting them out.

That's a pretty serious charge. A judge is in the unique situation to be able to right a wrong before things get out of hand. On the other hand, the judge also has to distinguish between a serious complaint of falling asleep on the job and an irrational complaint by a defendant who won't accept anything short of acquittal as satisfactory.

What to do? What to do, indeed. This particular body of law is often labeled a *Krankel* issue. It comes from an older Illinois Supreme Court decision that tried to outline how a judge should handle complaints from a defendant that his attorney did not do a good job. See *People v. Jolly*, 2014 IL 117142 (December), citing *People v. Krankel*, 102 Ill. 2d 181 (1984). In one way or another this will always be something trial judges have to grapple with.

So it's not a surprise that the process continues to be tweaked. The defendant will continue to make the complaints, so the court system will have plenty of chances to look at how they deal with this issue.

PEOPLE V. FLEMMING

So let's look at some cases that help us determine exactly what should happen after a defendant makes a claim of ineffective assistance of counsel. Let's begin with a murder trial where the defendant loses the trial.

https://IllinoisCaseLaw.com/018

At the sentencing hearing, the defendant brings up a *pro se* motion of ineffective assistance of counsel. It's quite typical that these complaints are brought up after a trial but before the sentencing hearing. Before the trial, the defendant's fate is still in the air and still being worked out. So it makes sense that after the trial is the time for a defendant to make the *pro se* motion saying his attorney sucked.

Also at a sentencing hearing, the judge will address the defendant and ask him if he wants to make a statement. A defendant chomping at the bit may take this opportunity to tell the judge what he really thinks about his counsel's performance.

In the case at hand, the exact allegations were that the counsel failed to present evidence on the victim's prior violence or the victim's prior aggressive behavior. The defendant also complained about his theory of self defense and how it wasn't laid out completely by the attorney. He also said his attorney never told him the victim was stabbed 6 times as opposed to only 3 times which is what the defendant thought. In any event, those were the claims.

In this case *People v. Flemming*, 2014 IL App (1st) 111925 (August), the judge right away goes to the state and asks the prosecutor to cross examine the defense attorney on this issue. Sure enough, the assistant state's attorney asks the defense attorney some questions on these topics. Defense counsel answers the questions, and the court is satisfied with the answers. The judge is so satisfied with the response that in that moment he denies the defendant's motion for a finding that the defense counsel was ineffective.

From the defendant's perspective it felt like they were ganging up on him. The prosecutor, the judge, and even his own attorney all came out against him. The issue on appeal was whether or not a full blown adversarial hearing had taken place before the defendant was appointed a new attorney. If a full blown hearing had transpired, that was a problem.

The body of law as set out in *People v. Krankel* established a two-step procedure for a trial court to follow when these complaints are brought up. The second part of the process involves what is called a full blown *Krankel* Hearing. The *Krankel* Hearing is an adversarial process were the state takes a side against the defendant. In a *Krankel* Hearing, the judge listens to evidence to decide if, in fact, the defense attorney was indeed negligent or ineffective. Often, the only witnesses are the defendant and the trial attorney. The defendant has to have a new attorney for the *Krankel* Hearing because we can't expect the criticized attorney (the trial attorney) to argue that he or she was, indeed, ineffective. That's just a bad idea. But in a *Krankel* Hearing you also have a prosecutor who ends up arguing that the defense attorney was not ineffective. Needless to say, if a judge believes a full blown adversarial *Krankel* Hearing is required, he has to dismiss the defense trial attorney and appoint a new attorney for the defendant.

The first step, as you can guess, is when the judge decides if a full blown hearing is even required in the first place. Most of these decisions focus on the first step, and mastering this step for most attorneys and judges will prove extremely useful. So we will focus and concentrate on the first step, and learn the law for the first step.

The first step is what happens immediately after the defendant first raises the claim that his attorney did a poor job. It's almost always going to be an oral motion. It can be written as well, rarely but sometimes they come to court with a new attorney already hired, and the new attorney is making the motion before the court. In this first step the judge is just gathering the information and the facts. It makes more sense to call the first step a *Krankel* Inquiry and keep the name *Krankel* Hearing for the full blown adversarial hearing, the second step.

Anyway, in the first step the judge is trying to decide two things. First, the judge is trying to decide whether or not he should just dismiss the complaint at that point by disregarding it as being frivolous or a strategic decision by trial counsel. If the judge finds that he can't dismiss the complaint as frivolous or a trial strategy then he or she has to decide if they are going to appoint a new attorney and continue the matter for the full blown *Krankel* Hearing. If it gets to this point, trial counsel is allowed to withdraw. Almost always, if a judge feels a complaint has merit and there is no strategic reason for the trial attorney's action or inaction, then new counsel will likely be appointed and the matter set over for a full hearing.

The thing to know about this first step, the *Krankel* Inquiry, is that there is no formal method or procedure as to how the judge conducts the step. There is no exact formula that the court has to follow to gather the information to make the decision that they need to make.

The judge does not always need to question anybody. Sometimes the judge has seen enough throughout the entire process to know what to do. Sometimes the defendant supplies enough information for the judge to rule with no other input required from the attorneys.

The judge is obviously allowed to ask questions of anyone involved that the court believes could help shed light on the issues being raised by the defendant. This almost always includes questioning and probing a little bit further into the defendant's allegations. The defendant should expect to get some clarification questions from the judge. The judge may want to hear from the defense attorney, who usually is standing right there, right next to the defendant when the first complaint is made.

Every once in a while, the prosecution could get some questions from the judge. This could happen if the defendant is making an allegation that revolves around an offer that was made or not made or not accurately related to the defendant or something like that, you never know. This is the *Krankel* Inquiry phase and all that is going on is the judge is doing his or her homework to gather the facts.

At this point, still the first step, the state's participation should be *de minimis* or probably be absolutely zero. The state essentially has no role here. The beef is between the defendant and his attorney. This has to just play out in front of them. They are just standing there waiting to see how it plays out. If the judge has questions for them, well then they'll answer them.

The problem with the case at hand is that the prosecutor got a little too involved by being the one who was cross-examining the defense attorney like he was his own witness. The appellate court said the prosecution should not have gotten involved like that, and still found this level of participation was *de minimis*. The court said that the question-answer format employed by the prosecutor with the defense attorney was not a full blown adversarial proceeding because nobody was making any substantive arguments. It was obvious here that the court was still gathering the facts and, although imprudently, relied on the prosecution to flush out the details. It was no different had the judge just asked the questions of the defense counsel.

At the first stage, the *Krankel* Inquiry is where we can nip many of these problems in the bud, and this is where we prevent misinformed allegations of ineffective assistance from progressing. It requires knowing the difference between a *Krankel* Inquiry and a *Krankel* Hearing and it means keeping your cool long enough for the trial judge to do his or her thing. The biggest mistake any attorney can make at the first step is to say too much. When you get a little hot-headed and long-winded, your comments easily turn into argumentative persuasion and you've crossed a line.

So now you know the general framework for how a judge should handle a defendant who has some complaining to do. The judge is going to have to do the old *Krankel* Two-Step. One thing is for sure, we'll never have a shortage of defendants complaining about their attorney, so we'll always have an opportunity to develop this body of law.

PEOPLE V. BOOSE

I have another case to mention that adds a different twist to our understanding. This time it's *People v. Boose*, 2014 IL App (2d) 130810 (September). You can catch the 13-minute recap of this case below:

https://IllinoisCaseLaw.com/019

We already talked about how the attorneys have very limited roles during the *Krankel* Inquiry. That's the point. They need to shut up and let the defendant have his moment. If there is a role to be played here by the attorneys, it is just to make sure the judge is making a clear record for any action that they may take. If a judge outright dismisses the initial complaint, the attorneys can confirm that the judge made clear what facts they relied on in making the ruling. If the judge is dismissing complaints and it's not clear on what grounds, the attorneys can step in to ask for clarification for the record.

In *Boose*, the opinion came out differently, so that gives us a great opportunity to distinguish and understand the differences. Here we have another defendant who loses the trial. This time it was a trial for violation of an order of protection. At the sentencing hearing, the defendant tells the judge that he has numerous complaints about the performance of his trial attorney. Some of these complaints were that the trial counsel failed to admit into evidence a CD that would have shown that the victim in the case called the defendant and was the aggressor.

He further complained that the state failed to prove that there was bodily harm in this case and that the defense attorney never made any arguments to show that the state never proved bodily harm. Defendant was complaining that his attorney became way too unprofessional, was verbally abusive, and attacked the prosecutor when the prosecutor mentioned that the defendant's own kids didn't like him. The defendant also complained about the fact that the defense attorney failed to inform the court how vindictive the prosecution was towards to the defendant.

Remember, the job of the trial court at this point is to let the defendant get his complaints out hassle-free. The judge then decides to dismiss outright as frivolous, dismiss as trial strategy, or advance the complaint to a full hearing. If the dismissal is not appropriate, that means new counsel must be appointed and the matter proceeds to a full blown Krankel Hearing. Here, the judge indeed dismissed all these complaints. That may not be too surprising.

I want to repeat some of the words said by the judge in dismissing these allegations. I just want you to get a feel for the judge's frame of mind. The trial judge said:

> "All the points were addressed. I did not find a scintilla of evidence that would support your claim of ineffective assistance. On behalf of defense counsel, who was a very seasoned defense attorney, gave you good representation. And, frankly, I can't believe

anything you are saying. They disproved you. The record disproves you. Nice try. That is all I can tell you."

Ouch. Clearly, the trial judge made the decision to dismiss all of these complaints outright because the court court believed they were frivolous.

So the question is why did the appellate court remand the case for a new *Krankel* Inquiry? Why did the appellate court say the trial court did something wrong?

As we get into the appellate court decision, it's helpful to go back and look at the allegations made against the attorney. How would you have felt if it was you in court when all these allegations were being made? How would you have reacted? What would you have thought if you were told you failed to admit a CD that showed the victim was angry at the defendant?

No doubt, the defense attorney was fuming due to the fact that the existence of the CD was detrimental to the client's own case. The charge was a violation of an order of protection. If the state could establish any contact between defendant and the victim they win. Obviously, counsel didn't admit the CD of their conversation. Duh!

If counsel had admitted it, no doubt the client would have alleged that was ineffective. The client was mad because the state didn't prove any bodily harm, and the defense attorney just sat by and let that go on. The charge is violation of order of protection. Bodily harm is not an element of the offense. The state doesn't have to prove bodily harm! That had to drive the attorney nuts.

If you were the attorney, wouldn't you have wanted to turn to the defendant and say,

> "The charge is violation of order of protection, not battery. It doesn't do you any good to have me standing up arguing that there was no bodily harm in this case. That doesn't defend you in any way. You're saying I was unprofessional when I got little heated with the prosecutor for telling the judge that your own kids don't like you? I was defending you. I was literally standing up for you and being a zealous advocate on your behalf. I don't know how you can think I did this in error!"

Maybe the defendant was thinking that by pissing off the prosecutor they now were going to come at him more aggressively, or maybe he thought he would lose a good offer. Who knows what the defendant was thinking.

Maybe he thought the charges were now not going to get dismissed since his attorney stood up for him. Who knows? But put yourself in the defense attorney's shoes. That attorney was out there advocating, probably for a real unlikeable guy, and now he's saying counsel is ineffective?

Prosecutors. What if you were the assistant state's attorney assigned to the case, and you're standing there when the defendant is telling the judge that you were vindictive towards the defendant? Are you going to stand there and let the defendant infer that you were anything other than professional in your handling of the prosecution against the defendant in this case?

It must have been hard for the prosecutor to not interrupt and say:

> "Vindictive? All I'm doing, sir, is upholding the law of this state. Just because you were charged with a violation of order of protection doesn't mean that I was being vindictive. I was following the rules, and I was following the law. Trying to win a conviction against someone who is clearly guilty doesn't rise to vindictiveness."

These quotes were not the exact quotes repeated in court. But, as you can imagine, it must have been really hard for the attorneys to just stand there and take it from the defendant. In many ways, this tension will always be there anytime a defendant is raising claims that he was wronged.

The appellate court reversed and remanded for a new *Krankel* Inquiry because the attorneys and the judge all did gang up against the defendant. They all got too argumentative and too defensive during the part that is simply designed for fact-gathering. When the complaint is first raised it's only a fact-finding procedure that takes place. Much more than that happened here.

Any scintilla of argument by an attorney is improper because it forces the defendant to defend the claim he is making against his lawyer. At that point, he is, essentially, lawyerless at the exact moment when he really needs a lawyer most.

Officially, the ruling was that the prosecution was granted an expanded role when they had an opportunity to contribute to the fact-gathering. That's when they became argumentative.

But looking back at it you can imagine that the defense attorney probably got some licks in as well. The lesson here for all of us working in a criminal court is that when these claims first come up you have to limit your responses to just the facts. You've got to limit your response to fact-finding. You can't become too argumentative. Even if the prosecution remains mute, if you are the one making arguments for your own effectiveness, that's crossing a line. That's a no-no.

Now you are arguing against your own client, and it can't happen. The judge has to gather the facts and it's up to the judge to dismiss outright if the court sees fit, and all you can do is make sure the judge has all the facts. That can be hard sometimes. If you're a good litigator, biting your tongue is not your first instinct. *Boose* does a better job of putting us in the moment and does a better job of making us reflect on exactly how we respond when these types of claims are brought up against us. It's the most frivolous claims, the ones that are most obviously ridiculous, and the ones that are most unfounded where you have to be the most careful. Those are the ones that are going to raise your internal heat temperature and cause you to blow your lid. But you have to calm down and follow the rules.

We all have a duty to make sure these cases don't come back and especially not come back because you got too argumentative too early. The non-frivolous claims will always be mixed in with the frivolous claims. The rules exist so that the defendant has a chance to express his sensation that counsel did not defend him adequately. We don't want baseless claims to advance beyond the first step, but even more damaging would be a situation where a defendant has a valid beef against his attorney but can't express his complaint cogent enough before getting attacked from all sides.

So we've been talking about the *Krankel* Two-Step which involves The *Krankel* Inquiry and the *Krankel* Hearing. By now you know the judge has to decide in the first step if they are going to dismiss a defendant's complaints based on being a frivolous claim or a matter of trial strategy. This is the initial inquiry that has to be considered by the court. Sometimes it's not so obvious that the defendant is officially making a claim against his attorney's effectiveness.

PEOPLE V. AYRES

This comes up in the case of *People v. Ayres*, 2017 IL 120162 (February), where we get to ask: "Exactly what does defendant have to say to trigger a *Krankel* Inquiry?" The other way to think about this question is: "What is the minimum a defendant has to say to put the court on notice that trial counsel may have been ineffective?"

In this case, the defendant files a *pro se* written motion that is mailed in. He was not in court and in person before the judge when he tried to raise a claim of his attorney's ineffectiveness. He basically said in the motion that his attorney was ineffective. That's it. That's all he says. He doesn't spell it out anymore beyond that, and just says, "my attorney was ineffective." No more details are provided.

That written motion gets ignored by the court. Nothing happens. It comes up on appeal where the issue was that the defendant raised a claim of ineffectiveness that was ignored by the trial judge. The defendant is saying the written motion should have at least provided a *Krankel* Inquiry where he was brought back into court to be asked by the judge what his beef was. The judge should have asked him more questions about his claim of ineffectiveness and given him an opportunity to flush this out.

The prosecution said, and I'm paraphrasing here,

> "No, you didn't even properly raise a *Krankel* issue. You gotta do more than just make a barenaked claim of ineffectiveness. You have to put some meat on that ineffectiveness bone, man. You didn't really put the court on notice that you are contesting anything. Thus, you never really raised an issue and the trial court was right to ignore the motion."

The Illinois Supreme Court jumped in to help clarify exactly what has to be said to start a legit *Krankel* Inquiry. The court now says that a barenaked allegation of ineffective assistance of counsel is sufficient to raise the issue and put the trial court on notice that they must fish out additional affirmation by conducting a first-step *Krankel* Inquiry.

It was error in this case for the trial judge not to have transported the defendant back to court to inquire about his complaint. The high court explained that the whole point of a *Krankel* Inquiry is to flush out the issue. The trial judge needs to make sure that they are gathering the facts and forming a record so that the higher courts don't have to spend years and decades litigating something that could have been taken care of at the trial level.

That's the whole point of the *Krankel* Inquiry and the *Krankel* Hearing. If they created a rule that required the defendant to do more than just state a barenaked allegation then appellate courts would just end up litigating the issue down the road which is what they are trying to prevent.

The trial judge knew enough to know that he or she should have brought the defendant back to court to ask more questions. The case got reversed and remanded back to the trial judge so he or she could do just that.

What happens if the judge appoints a different attorney who conducts a *Krankel* Hearing, and the judge finds the original counsel was derelict? Well, the judge would have have to order a new trial at that point. The Illinois Supreme Court would prefer for all of this to happen at the trial level. There's no point in pushing a case through just so that an appellate court could reverse and remand for a new trial years or decades later.

I think it's fair to say this decision has set a low threshold for investigating claims of ineffective of counsel. This is true for all the reasons stated above. We don't want to make it impossible for defendants to have their issues addressed at the trial level just so that an appellate court can look at the issue down the road.

On the other hand, I think it's also fair to say that the defendant has some obligation to make sure he is effectively making an understandable claim against his attorney's performance. A client who gets up there with pure hate, anger, and disagreement could risk not being clear in his beef against his attorney.

I never thought I'd be saying this, but sometimes a clarifying question may be required.

> "Yes, John. We can see that you're pissed at the world, the victim, the jury, the judge, and the prosecution. But did your attorney do anything wrong?"

I'll let you use that question at your own discretion.

PEOPLE V. BROWN

I'll tell you right now, the attorneys that get the most of this material will be the ones who can be reflective about the content.

Attorneys who can imagine being in the situations described here are the ones who will be able to envision their own performance in similar situations. The attorneys who immediately thought of that time a client said this or that about them in court now have the analysis from the cases with which to better evaluate what happened to them. This is a broader lesson that rings especially true for the attorneys who are regular subscribers and listeners to the Premium Nuggets Podcast.

The more attorneys can ask themselves what they would have done in the situation, the better off those attorneys will be the next time.

What did you do the last time a client started bad-mouthing you in court? How did the judge react? What would you do differently if that happened today?

These are the kinds of thought processes that make the listeners better in court. Case after case, episode after episode, they just get smarter and better. Continuing on with this *Krankel* issues, one may ask:

> *"What would I do or should I do if
> I know I made a mistake and my client
> actually has a legitimate complaint against me?"*

Well, when you read enough cases, eventually, you begin to see everything. Interestingly, I came across the case of *People v. Brown*, 2017 IL App (3d) 140921 (June). If you have a moment and a browser, you can listen to the 7-minute audio summary of this case by hitting the link below (you can tell I was a little more confident behind the microphone this time):

https://IllinoisCaseLaw.com/383

This case was a domestic battery prosecution. The victim testified that the defendant was mad at her. They were arguing. She said he hit her and choked her. Defendant gets on the stand and completely denies that anything happened. He is found guilty, and right away before they even get to a sentencing hearing, the defendant is telling the judge that his attorney did not defend him to the best of her ability.

He said the attorney did not call two of his witnesses that were there and who saw the whole thing and who would have testified that none of it happened. The defense attorney fesses up. She accepts responsibility. She tells the judge (paraphrasing here):

> "Yeah, you know what, judge? He did tell me about these two witnesses. I will confess to that. At the time I was never able to find any addresses for them or other information about them. Then it got away from me. I should have dug deeper into identifying and locating the witnesses."

The attorney then, essentially, was conceding her own ineffectiveness and agreed with the defendant's motion against her.

She asks that the court consider the verdict and set it aside on the basis that the jurors didn't hear all the information. It was just a miscommunication, she said. But the miscommunication led to the defendant not being able to call the witnesses who could exonerate him. He did not have the best case that he could have had had she followed through and located the witnesses. Her bad. She took the blame.

This is definitely a weird situation. You have an attorney who is essentially arguing for her own ineffectiveness. What should a court do with that? There are different things to consider. On one hand, we may want to praise the attorney for stepping up and taking the heat and acknowledging her mistake. The defendant should not be harmed because counsel slipped up. Yet it's easy to see why we wouldn't want to give too much credence or weight to attorneys who start falling on their swords.

The incentives in that case would get all screwy. All of a sudden we would have attorneys falling on their swords left and right if they thought it would get their clients a new trial. Some attorneys would do it maliciously. That is, they would purposely not do something or do something wrong thinking they'd just get a do-over if it doesn't work out for them. Other attorneys may just needlessly fall on their sword thinking that it would help the client even though they thought they did everything they could do for the client. So you can see the genuine dilemma a judge is confronted with when this comes up.

In this case, the trial judge denied the motion and found there was no ineffective assistance of counsel. The trial judge found that the lawyer didn't do anything wrong. The defendant never told her how to find or reach the witnesses. The problem here was not the attorney but the defendant who withheld key information from his attorney.

The appellate court also recognizes the dilemma that these situations create. The appellate court made it clear there is no *per se* rule of ineffectiveness any time a trial attorney is admitting they were ineffective. What does this mean? It means trial judges don't have to listen to attorneys who are admitting error. The trial judge should run the same analysis that they would otherwise run, giving no special weight to the attorneys proclamation that, "I screwed up."

In the *Krankel* scenario it just means the judge runs the same *Krankel* Inquiry. The judge independently determines if there is cause to deny the motion for ineffectiveness. Even if the judge ends up agreeing with the defendant that the attorney possibly errored, it just means new counsel needs to be appointed and a full blown *Krankel* Hearing must be run where the outcome may be different.

Logically, this makes sense. We can't start granting new trials every time an attorney says he or she did something wrong. All of a sudden you'd see attorneys stepping up and professing error to benefit the client.

In the above case, the reviewing court said that if the trial attorney really wanted to show that her client was prejudiced by not calling these witnesses, she would have had to done much more than just confess error. She needed to hunt down the witnesses for the court. She needed an affidavit with some leg work. At a minimum, she needed to establish that these witnesses were located and subject to being subpoenaed. Saying "I committed error, and I hurt my client" was not enough. She did not establish her client was actually prejudiced.

Practically, a judge is likely to just dismiss the attorney and appoint a new attorney and move on to a full-blown adversarial hearing. Unless, of course, if an attorney makes a ridiculous claim of their own ineffectiveness the judge will then dismiss the complaint outright. None of that happened here. The case was remanded so that the judge could appoint the new attorney.

For us attorneys, the list of complaints from our clients about the things we did or did not do in their case will certainly feature not hunting down and calling witnesses. This we know, and this is a given. When a client mentions a witness or "someone that was there," in our own heads alarm bells need to be going off. That has to be something we look into. Either an alibi witness is being described or a post trial issue is being raised that will need to be put to bed. Either way, the trial attorney has work to do. Said differently, if you don't track down that possible witness, that is something for darn sure the client will complain about later, and you'll have some explaining to do at a later date.

Maybe all you end up doing is creating a memo to yourself that you put in your file outlining how the witness told you something completely different than what your client told you. Whatever the reason, you backup your file and cover your behind. If you get called on why crazy witness X was never called as a witness you'll have a response.

I probably don't need to say this, but let me spell it out. Falling on your sword is never a good litigation strategy. It's not good for anyone. It's certainly not good for your client if you are not advocating to your best ability all the time. It's not good for your reputation as a criminal litigator to be known as the attorney who confesses error after every trial.

The court ain't going to do you or your client any favors in the situation where you genuinely have to confess error. You'll still have to prove exactly how and why you messed up and that you prejudiced your client in one way or another.

Our court system does recognize certain automatic errors. But when an attorney stands up to confess their own ineffectiveness the court will not automatically find that the attorney was actually ineffective. The defendant is still going to have to prove and establish the ineffectiveness.

This case, *Brown*, does a great job of reminding us that we have to be on our toes all the time before trial, during trial, and after trial. The slackers have no advantage. We must do our best all the time. The advantage goes to the attorney who is the sharpest.

SECTION SEVEN: DOUBLE JEOPARDY TIPS, TRICKS, AND LITIGATION TACTICS

One clear advantage of listening to the cases regularly is that you finally get to go on an offensive footing with the cases. What do I mean by that?

Well, usually we dive into case law when it's being used against us in court. That's not a real productive way to learn the case. Sure, you have to read the thing and understand it, and of course you would have learned something, but your mental frame was all defense oriented. Similarly, even when you casually read through the cases or your case digest to "get ahead", there is a mental tax associated with hunting down the material and sifting slowly through it.

The episodes in the Premium Nuggets Podcast concisely present the case law that regular listeners are able to effortlessly digest. Regular listeners to the case law episodes released on the Premium Nuggets Podcast are digesting the material for the first time in a fresh, concise manner. It means they can start to think of the cases offensively. They are pulling out only the most important parts of the cases and assimilating the material into their already existing litigation arsenal. This is what I mean when I say listeners quickly learn to explode their litigation skills and tactics.

PEOPLE V. GUILLEN

Double jeopardy is a great example of what I mean. It is a fundamental concept in the criminal law. It's something we read about in law school and maybe have seen in a few hearings in court. Certainly, we've all seen it applied in the movies.

Most attorneys however aren't thinking of double jeopardy as a tool in their litigation belt. It's not a concept with developed automatic litigation protocols. It wasn't until I started reading and reporting the cases that I could think differently about such a basic concept as double jeopardy. This can be true for listeners as well. The idea is to reintroduce the subject matter in a way that it is internalized, remembered, and added to the litigation arsenal.

With a just a few cases, a litigator can have this concept reconfigured in his or her mind and ready to implement in court. The case of *People v. Guillen*, 2014 IL App (2d) 131216 (November) is a great start. The audio report on this case can be found at the link below:

https://IllinoisCaseLaw.com/040

The case began when the defendant was in court with his attorney trying to quash a DUI warrant. The warrant gets quickly removed and defendant gets motivated to plead guilty to the charge all in the same day. However, the prosecutor and defense attorney can't come up with agreed-upon terms. They don't agree with the factual basis and don't even agree on the applicable sentence.

Needless to say, it looked like it would have to be a cold plea. The defendant was ready to just plead guilty before the judge and was ready to let the judge sentence him. It doesn't even look like either side was aware that defendant was eligible for a felony enhancement due to a prior DUI. It didn't look like the defense attorney was trying to get a plea as quickly as possible before the other side decided to enhance the charges. But that sometimes happens.

Sometimes you see your client is charged with a misdemeanor when you know he is eligible for far way more serious charges. In these situations, there may be an advantage to pleading guilty to the lesser charge and locking it in before the state has a chance to raise the charges. This is actually one litigation strategy that relies on the principle of double jeopardy. The idea is that once your client pleads guilty to a misdemeanor, double jeopardy is what would kick in to prevent the state from bringing more serious, charges against your client. There is nothing illegal or illegitimate about that. It's just how it works.

It doesn't look like this is what was happening in this case. I say that because the defense attorney would not have negotiated so vigorously with the prosecution if they just wanted to lock in the misdemeanor. There would have been no point in bringing the case to their attention. They could have just gone right to the judge and plead guilty.

Eventually, the defendant and his attorney make it back in front of the judge. They proceed to plead guilty to a misdemeanor DUI without an agreement with the prosecution on the sentencing. The judge finishes all his admonishments to the defendant, and it appeared like the judge had accepted the guilty plea from defendant.

But before the hearing finishes, the prosecutor realizes that the defendant was in fact eligible for a felony. In those moments, right before the judge tells the defendant his sentence, the prosecutor interrupts the judge and informs the judge that he thinks this guy is enhanceable. The prosecutor tells the judge he wants to dismiss the misdemeanor charge, and he doesn't want to go through the plea and sentencing anymore. The judge grants his motion to dismiss the charges. The defendant is, in fact, later charged with an aggravated DUI which is an enhanced felony charge.

The issue on appeal was whether or not the defendant was subjected to double jeopardy during the misdemeanor hearing when he was tried and thought he was pleading guilty to the misdemeanor DUI. In other words, did the defendant essentially plead guilty in the first hearing such that double jeopardy would prevent the state from bringing additional charges based on the same conduct?

This is a very interesting case because it gets to the very root of the meaning of double jeopardy. It allows us to get into the very basic fundamentals of this law. We all know about double jeopardy from law school.

Generally, we understand a person can't be twice put in jeopardy of life or limb. See U.S. Const., amend. V. See also Ill. Const. 1970, art. I, § 10; 720 ILCS 5/3-4. So you can't face jeopardy twice for the same conduct.

The question then becomes how do we know when a person has faced jeopardy the first time? Before we prevent jeopardy a second time we have to be sure the person faced it a first time.

For example, we say in a jury trial setting that jeopardy attaches when a jury is impaneled and sworn in. So you've picked them, and you've sworn them all in. The case law is quite clear and specific that no testimony needs to be heard for jeopardy to attach. It's the swearing in that is crucial. That's when an individual has been put in jeopardy of life or limb for an offense.

Actually, a lot has happened. The defendant likely has been arrested. He's probably had a bail set. He's likely been to court on numerous pretrial hearings. But it isn't until trial day when they pick and swear in a jury when the law says he was ever in any real jeopardy. When that happens, that's when it gets real for the defendant. That's when he knows he's in trouble. But our case was not a jury nor a bench trial. We have a guilty plea.

Here the case law is a little bit more fuzzy. We have an opinion from the Illinois Supreme Court that says jeopardy can attach in a plea-sentencing hearing when the court accepts the plea. That's all they say. They don't get into a definition of the term "accepts," and they don't flush it out. They just leave it at that. When a plea is accepted, jeopardy has attached. If we just accept this for what it is, we know that in a plea-sentencing hearing, jeopardy will attach sometime after the plea but before an actual sentence is given.

The appellate court in this case, for all intents and purposes, put the discretion of accepting the guilty plea into the hands of the trial court. The appellate court essentially granted the trial judge the authority to vacate a guilty plea before sentencing without having to worry about jeopardy. They completely put it in the hands of the trial judge. Again, on its face this really isn't a bad thing. In the opinion, they explain that we want judges to have this discretion.

In a plea-sentencing hearing the judge is gathering all the facts and compiling all the relevant information about the case. The judge should have the time to gather the information he or she needs. If the judge comes up with information in that process that is worrisome we want them to have the discretion to stop, cancel, vacate or undo the plea-sentencing hearing without the judge having to worry about jeopardy attaching. This is a good thing.

In the end, the appellate court said that the defendant in this case never really faced any meaningful jeopardy nor could he expect any degree of finality merely from the fact that the judge began to discuss the sentencing issues. The appellate court acknowledged that it looked and felt like a plea and sentencing hearing, but this defendant never faced any real jeopardy from a hearing that was essentially canceled by the judge. Sure, the judge was prompted by the prosecution to stop the hearing. At the end of the day, the judge has to make the call. Often, it is the parties who are providing the important details of a case to the judge. The prosecution's motion to dismiss doesn't mean that the judge acquiesced his or her authority to terminate the hearing.

The dissent makes some good points that can help us understand what the majority was thinking. The dissent said that the majority opinion sounds nice and it looks logical. The problem was that the facts that were before the appellate court didn't fit the situation that the appellate court was describing. What they were talking about, all that legal mumbo jumbo, might have been applicable under a different set of facts and circumstances.

But that wasn't the scenario this appellate panel was dealing with. They had different facts before them. There was nothing preliminary about the plea-sentencing hearing that the defendant found himself in. Any neutral outside observer looking down at the hearing would not have found that a preliminary fact finding hearing was being conducted by the court. It would have appeared to be a real plea in every way.

What is missing from the majority opinion is the perspective from the defendant's vantage point. From the defendant's viewpoint, he had every reason to think he was in full jeopardy. He was standing in a misdemeanor courtroom, facing a misdemeanor charge, and telling the judge that he did it. He was admonished by the court of his rights and told of the seriousness of the proceeding. He made statements in open court, and he was 100% reasonable in expecting that he would be sentenced for the charge. Who in their right mind can say that he didn't face jeopardy at that point? He was in jeopardy, plain and simple. Nothing happened that would have signaled to the defendant that the judge was still gathering facts and still in a preliminary mindset. This was not a practice run from the defendant's perspective. The trial judge had accepted the defendant's guilty plea in every sense of the word. True, he hadn't been sentenced yet, but that plea was accepted in every other sense and meaning of the word "accept."

The dissident's view is that the opinion in effect has moved the goalposts. The Supreme Court had held that jeopardy attaches after a guilty plea. This opinion appears to have moved jeopardy to some point after sentencing which was not previously the law of the land.

One of the fascinating things about this case is that the outcome could have easily been different with different judges. Mix around the panel of judges at the appellate court, and it's easy to see a different result. Had a different trial judge heard the case in the first place, he or she would have been persuaded at the trial level that jeopardy had attached at the original plea-sentencing hearing.

Guillen was a great case to introduce us to the concept and a great case to begin to help us frame double jeopardy with a new fresh offensive footing. Before leaving *Guillen*, we can still get a little more mileage out of it. This is one of the advantages of dissecting the cases with an offensive mindset.

Sometimes an issue might require revisiting it to make sure all the kinks are ironed out. That's why I recorded an additional podcast on this topic. To get up to speed you can listen by following the link below:

https://IllinoisCaseLaw.com/041

Had the defendant won the issue, it would have prevented the state from charging him with the more serious felony aggravated DUI charge. Had the court said that the defendant was in jeopardy after he plead guilty, that would have meant no other charge could have been made against the defendant. That's the point of double jeopardy, it prevents the second conviction for the same offense.

No doubt the appellate court judges had this in the back of their minds when they made their decision. Had they found that jeopardy had attached it, not only would that have meant that the defendant could not have been charged with the felony DUI, it also would have meant that he could not have been recharged with the misdemeanor DUI.

Remember, the original misdemeanor DUI was dismissed after he plead guilty to it but before he was sentenced. So had the defendant won the issue, it would have meant he couldn't be recharged with anything. He would have been unchargeable. This was a defendant who was in warrant status for a long time before he finally showed up to court in the first place. I'm pretty sure this is something that was pressing on the minds of the appellate court judges and something that they took into account.

This brings us to a deeper issue that we can look at. Now we can explore questions like, "Why do we even have a rule against double jeopardy in the first place? Why does this rule exist? What is it trying to protect?"

It's not an easy question to answer. No instinctual response is forthcoming. The smart people who have looked at these questions have come up with this: Double jeopardy is two sides of one coin. There are two main equally important principles that are at play when we talk about why we have this rule.

The first one is to prevent any type of prosecutorial overreach or prosecutorial abuse. It's clearly a restraint on the state. The ability to lock people up is a powerful thing. And one goal of the rule against double jeopardy is to prevent the state from getting carried away.

On the other side of the coin we have protection of the defendant. We want to protect the defendant from having to face numerous or multiple prosecutions for the same offense. We don't want a defendant to be punished more than once for the same crime. We don't want a defendant who is acquitted to be tried again and go through another ordeal.

When I say it's the other side of the same coin I say that because it's hard to say which is more important. Is it more important to prevent governmental overreach, or is it more important to protect defendants? They are both valuable goals and important principles. Both of these ideas comprise the major reasons why we have a rule against double jeopardy.

Understanding these principles can in turn help us understand other aspects of double jeopardy. For example, why don't we just say that jeopardy attaches after an actual verdict or finding of guilty? In a bench trial, jeopardy attaches when the first witness is sworn in. That is sooner than an actual verdict. In a jury trial, the rule is that jeopardy attaches after the jury is sworn in. Again, that happens much sooner than a verdict. During a plea setting jeopardy attaches when the judge accepts the plea.

We can think through these rules by thinking about the scenario differently. Let's imagine a world where the rules are different, where jeopardy only attaches after a guilty verdict from a jury or guilty finding from a judge. In this world, before that point we say no jeopardy attaches. The lines are drawn arbitrarily.

Judges just made them up. Judges just started saying, "Ok, jeopardy attaches here and not there." In the imaginary world where jeopardy attaches only after a verdict, the two rationales for having the rule would be completely undermined. The principles on this mythical coin could not be enhanced or advanced in any way.

Imagine a world where prosecutors could bring a charge, put on witnesses, and almost finish the trial before it becomes clear that their case sucks. If the prosecution felt their case was tanking, they could just dismiss the charges and refile after buffing up their case. If the rule was that jeopardy didn't attach because the jury didn't reach a verdict, nothing would prevent the prosecution from doing this over and over again until they thought they got it right. In that world, there is no real restraint on the prosecution and no real protection for defendants.

If we believe that both sides of the coin have principles worth advancing and believing in, then the rule has to be that jeopardy attaches before a verdict is reached. Exactly where is completely arbitrary, but we can see it has to be before a verdict is reached.

The next practical question is: Where should judges draw this jeopardy attachment line? Well, it can be drawn anywhere. The further you get from a verdict the more protection the defendant is being given and the more restraint is felt by the state. The closer you get to a verdict the less protection a defendant has precisely because the state has less restraint. You can see this by taking our imaginary world in the other direction.

Let's pretend the rule is that jeopardy attaches the moment a charge is filed. We can say that. Why not? This is our imaginary world. We can say the rule is that a defendant has faced jeopardy anytime charges have been filed against him. That means the state would not be able to dismiss charges and recharge later. They would be barred by double jeopardy from doing that. This would afford defendants much more protection, but it would be at the cost of tying the prosecution's hands, maybe too much.

We do want the state to have some flexibility in bringing charges, dropping charges, and bringing charges depending on the circumstances. If we say jeopardy attaches too soon, we would essentially be robbing the prosecutor from making appropriate charging decisions as facts, circumstances, and witnesses are developed.

There are times when the state believes it's appropriate to bring a charge, and then they evaluate the strength and conclude it's not as strong as they thought. We want them to drop a case to improve the investigation and still be able to bring the charges without any double jeopardy prohibitions.

The rules we dictate when jeopardy attaches is a compromise between the competing interests of the state and the defendant.

Let's get out of these imaginary worlds and come back to the real world. In the real world, the rules say that jeopardy does not attach until a jury is picked and sworn in, a witness is sworn in at a bench trial, or a judge accepts a plea at a hearing.

This means a person can be investigated, charged, go through pretrial motions and hearings, bond hearings, an evidentiary hearing or whatever, they could do all that and still jeopardy would not have attached against that defendant. The state would retain the flexibility to dismiss and walk away only to possibly bring charges in the future.

It's only after the swearing-in of the jury or a witness in a bench trial or the plea acceptance when we would acknowledge that the defendant has been put through the wringer. This is when we tell the state that if they dismiss, they won't be allowed to bring charges in the future.

We are telling the prosecution that they had all that time beforehand to investigate the case, strengthen their side, and be sure they wanted to proceed to a trial and verdict. This would include gathering all the information they need to make the appropriate charging decision in the first place. If they want to enhance or charge something more serious, they have to do it before the court accepts a plea on their current charges. If the prosecution hasn't decided to indict defendant with more serious charges before the jury is picked and sworn in, then by that point they have lost that opportunity to do that.

Jumping back to *Guillen*, the case that got us going on these ideas, we recall that case was a guilty plea situation. There was no trial. That defendant was charged, had a bond, and had a warrant all before he came back to court to plead guilty. The prosecution could have enhanced him at any time before he came in to plead guilty including the entire time he was in warrant status. But they decided to wait until the very moment that he plead guilty and before the judge sentenced him to dismiss so they could refile more serious charges.

When do we think they should have lost the right to do so? If there is some criticism against this ruling it's that they didn't take into account the other side of the coin. They didn't take into account any of the defendant's rights, interests, or protection that we say the rule against double jeopardy is supposed to protect.

The decision focuses on the judge being the one who gets to decide when a plea is accepted and when it's not, but the decision was, without knowing it, really promoting the state's right to dismiss and refile. Remember, had the court ruled differently, the prosecution wouldn't have been able to refile the more serious felony DUI charge. They also would not have been able to recharge the defendant on the misdemeanor. He would have gotten off scot-free.

On the Premium Nuggets Podcast I discuss fundamental ideas we talked about in law school. When listeners are grounded in the fundamentals, they are better prepared to instantly draw on those ideas when they encounter their application in court. You better believe a listener to the podcast is going to be telling the judge about how double jeopardy has two competing interests, and you can't ignore one to save the other other. When you have the fundamentals under your belt, other ideas instantly make sense.

PEOPLE V. STAPLE

Take for example what happened in *People v. Staple*, 2016 IL App (4th) 160061 (December). Like all the other episodes I've been citing here, this one is also open to the reader for easy listening. This episode was 9 minutes long.

https://IllinoisCaseLaw.com/279

The defendant has two charges of DUI filed against him at the same time. One is a misdemeanor, and the other one is a felony. This happens all the time. Officers use traffic citations to file the misdemeanor charges and prosecutors, a few days later, often bring the felony charges. Misdemeanors are typically filed under "DT" numbers with the clerk's office, and the felonies may have a "CF" number. Sometimes different file jackets are created for the same conduct, the same arrest, and for the same DUI.

Here, we don't know the reason two different files were created. Was it a clerical error? Or did the state mean to move everything into the CF and just never got around to it? The defendant pleads guilty to the misdemeanor in the DT file and then quickly moves the trial court to dismiss the felony charges based on double jeopardy concerns. He told the trial judge that since he already plead on the DT, the state is not allowed to get another conviction on the CF file, and they have to dismiss the more serious charges. Otherwise, he said he'll be punished twice for the same conduct. The trial judge looks at this and acknowledges the files and the law, and he is obviously versed in double jeopardy concerns. The judge then dismisses the felony charges in the CF file.

The prosecutor is left there with his mouth hanging open wondering what the the heck just happened. I'm sure he told the judge that he couldn't dismiss the felony just because the defendant plead to the lower count. Had these charges all been brought in the same file jacket, the court certainly would not dismiss the felony charges simply because the defendant plead guilty to the lesser offense and not guilty to the more serious offense.

The trial judge was not persuaded by the state and dismissed. On appeal, the central issue revolved around the meaning of double jeopardy and the appropriateness of applying it to these circumstances. Don't forget any of the material we already talked about. It's all important. It all has to go into are thinking.

In this case, we get a different recitation of the reasons why we have a prohibition against double jeopardy in this country. This case talks about three reasons rather than just two. Here they say the double jeopardy clause protects against:

> (1) A second prosecution for the same offense following acquittal,
> (2) A second prosecution for the same offense following conviction, and
> (3) Multiple punishments for the same offense.

These principles are entirely consistent with the two-sided coin we spoke of earlier. Those two sides were to prevent government overreaching and to protect defendants.

We can see that the first prong prevents the government from getting a second bite at the apple after they lose a case that has gone to a full verdict. In the second prong, after the state actually wins a conviction, we will then not allow them to double-dip to get a second conviction and punishment for the same conduct. The third prong is all about protecting the defendant and preventing multiple punishments for the same offense, but it's also tied to the first two prongs.

This case talks about the principles that double jeopardy is intended to prevent. The case also mentions this idea that double jeopardy was created as a shield and not intended to be used as a sword by defendants. We see this idea of "sword v. shield" come up in other areas of the criminal law.

Double jeopardy is there to protect the defendant and was not created to be used as a weapon by him. The law recognizes that double jeopardy is only intended to be used as a shield by a defendant and not used as a sword. It's there to protect defendants against prosecutorial overreach, and it's not really intended for defendants to be using it as a weapon to gut a case before it gets started by the prosecution.

Recall the clear language from other cases that double jeopardy is not to be applied in a strictly mechanical manner. Combine this with the idea that double jeopardy is a shield and not a sword, and we can see that double jeopardy should be applied sparingly. Especially in situations that don't implicate the special concerns, there the rule has no place. Purely mechanical application may frustrate society's ultimate interest in enforcing its goals and its criminal laws.

And that's all the prosecution was trying to explain to this judge. He was saying (I'm paraphrasing here), "Judge, take a step back and let's not apply this thing mechanically to our case. But let's look at the goals and interests that double jeopardy is supposed to be protecting, and let's see if they are even implicated in our situation."

Thinking about it this way, we could see that the prosecution could have brought all the charges under one file in one case jacket with numerous counts. We wouldn't let a defendant come into court and plead to the lesser counts in a CF file and then demand that the more serious counts be dismissed. Double jeopardy doesn't say that's okay. That is essentially what he did here.

He plead to the misdemeanor in the CM file and demanded the felony in the CF file be dismissed. When a defendant pleads to a lesser charge that's part of a more general prosecution, he has not been exposed to convictions on the higher charges. The state hasn't had a chance to marshal their case and bring forth the evidence that they say they have as it relates to the more serious charges.

Clearly, there has not been a trial on those issues. The case, in no serious way, has been tested in front of a jury. The defendant certainly hasn't been punished for a felony, so he can't say that he's now being punished twice for the same charge. None of the government overreaching that we are looking to constrain has happened nor is it implicated in any way.

The reviewing court reversed the dismissal and reinstated the more serious felony charges against the defendant. Admittedly, this case does feel similar to the first case. In *Guillen,* the case was all about not allowing the state to proceed with a felony after the defendant had plead guilty to the misdemeanor. That's exactly what happened here, isn't it?

Well, yes. The cases seem similar in form, but they are quite different in substance. Double jeopardy is not an absolute rule. Maybe there are some situations where a defendant pleads guilty to a CM, and the state tries to file some CF counts years or months later. This would be a situation where double jeopardy would step in to properly prevent the state from filing those additionally CF counts. But this is not that scenario.

In this case, the CM and the CF were filed simultaneously, and the defendant was always aware of the more serious counts. They were not filed months or years later and could not be considered a second prosecution. None of the concerns and worries that we have about prosecutorial overreach and protecting the defendant against multiple prosecutions were at play.

By not applying the prohibition mechanically, it means we allow for some situations where the state is allowed to file a CF charge after a CM charge has been filed. Here, the state was not trying to sneak additional charges past somebody. The defendant knew about them from the get-go. These charges might as well have all been in the same file number. Procedurally, it was as though all the charges were actually filed together in the same file jacket.

Inherently, we kind of know that double jeopardy is never applied mechanically. If it were, every time there was a reversal on a conviction at the appellate court, the higher court would never be allowed to remand for a new trial. If we applied the rule mechanically, we would say every time there was a reversal on an issue the charges would have to be dismissed and the defendant would have to be acquitted on the reversed counts. A mechanical application of double jeopardy would definitely prevent a second trial.

You ever notice after a reversal of a conviction how the appellate judges are sure to include a final paragraph saying they thought the case was proved beyond a reasonable doubt? What's that all about? Why do the judges do that? They do that because they are keenly aware that double jeopardy prevents a second prosecution against an individual who has been acquitted of the charges. Acquittal is just a finding of non-guilty.

So when they are saying there was sufficient evidence to convict they are basically saying that the defendant was not acquitted. If there is no acquittal the state is allowed to proceed with a second prosecution. They didn't have a weak case, so they are allowed a second bite at the apple. They had a sufficient case and could have won beyond a reasonable doubt but for the error in the case. Also, since they are reversing the conviction there are no "multiple convictions" to worry about. With that finding they can remand for a new trial and make everyone do it all over again.

Well then, if double jeopardy is not to be used as a sword and only as a shield, when can it ever be used offensively? That's a good question, and there are definitely good reasons to keep reading. Maybe another way to think about it is this way: "Are there trial settings I should familiarize myself with that could legitimately implicate double jeopardy concerns?" The answer to the second question is a firm "yes." Ignoring the final two cases means you may be disarming yourself in a trial when you face a scenario that could implicate double jeopardy. If you can't identify a problem as it's happening you won't know what to say or do to ensure a second prosecution is forbidden.

Similarly, if you are on the side of the prosecution, a keen understanding of double jeopardy fundamentals is important to ensure you don't accidentally or inadvertently knock yourself out of a second prosecution.

I'm fond of saying that a courtroom is a dangerous place. If that's true, a jury trial is downright deadly. Those attorneys best schooled in double jeopardy fundamentals will instantly know what's at stake when and if they ever face a mistrial.

PEOPLE V. THREATTE

Let's jump over and look at *People v. Threatte*, 2017 IL App (2d) 160161 (August). If you want to give your eyes a break and let your ears do some of the heavy lifting go to the url below:

https://IllinoisCaseLaw.com/389

This case does a great job of illustrating how knowing the fundamentals helps an attorney formulate arguments, be creative, and get the job done.

What we have in this case is a domestic battery trial. The prosecutor ends up getting sick in the middle of the trial. She has to go home, and we don't really learn the details of what was going on or what her illness was. It doesn't really matter. The point is that she could not continue with the trial. It was unknown how long she'd be out. Supervising prosecutors show up to court to tell the judge they don't know exactly what is going on with her. They know she was in a bad way, and that she couldn't be in court. They ask the judge to continue the case for 24 hours so that they could determine what was happening with her.

Bottom line is that they didn't know how long the assigned prosecutor would be out, and they wanted some time to figure it out. The judge wasn't sure how long he'd have to keep the jury on ice and instead decides to release the jury and declares a mistrial.

The issue for us to consider now is whether or not the state should be allowed to retry the defendant or should double jeopardy kick in to prevent a new trial.

Here's what the Constitution says about double jeopardy: "nor shall any person be subject for the same offense to be twice put in jeopardy for life or limb." U. S. Const. amend. V. There are three fundamental principles or reasons why we have the double jeopardy rule. I know we just discussed these principles but let me recite them again here so they get hammered into your head:

> (1) No second prosecution for the same offense following acquittal,
> (2) No second prosecution for the same offense following a conviction, and
> (3) No multiple punishments for the same offense.

I can't overstress how important the fundamentals are. If you know where the law comes from, you're dangerous in court.

The other way to think about these principles is to remember the outcome of a trial. There are only two outcomes. The state will win or lose.

If the prosecutors lose, that's an acquittal, and there is no second chance. If they win and get a conviction, they only get to do that once. No piling on for good measure. That's one way to think about it. Right off the bat in this case you can see right away that there is only one real legitimate concern.

There was no conviction in this case, so principle number 2 and number 3 are not in play. This case is, and you can even argue all mistrials are, all about the first prong. The main concern here is the idea that the court should try to prevent a second trial if there was an acquittal. I know what you're thinking. You're thinking there was no real acquittal either. The jury never actually got to deliberate and never came to a verdict.

But double jeopardy still has a role to play here. What we are asking ourselves is, "Was it likely there was going to be an acquittal?" If the state begins a trial it can't win double jeopardy should kick in to protect the defendant and prevent the prosecution from getting a second bite at the apple. Sometimes the state may have rushed to trial without all the facts. Other times the state's case may fall apart once they get started. Witnesses may unexpectedly start flipping on the prosecution and the case goes downhill after that.

Also, you may remember the rule that double jeopardy attaches after a jury is sworn in during a jury trial and when the first witness is sworn in during a bench trial. Well, both of those things have happened here so why wouldn't the rule just kick in to prevent a retrial? Good question.

Let's also not forget that the double jeopardy principles are never to be applied mechanically and without thought as to what is really going on. The rules we spoke about earlier dealt with a different scenario. The scenario dealt with what to do after a trial has started and then the state dismisses. That's a different circumstance than what we've got here. What we have here is a mistrial involving a prosecutor who got sick. Justice may not necessarily be served by blindly applying the "sworn in jury" and "sworn in witness" rules.

And while we are at it, let's also mention the principle that double jeopardy should only be used as a shield by defendants and shouldn't be used as a sword. That means we shouldn't give defendants a windfall and an easy win just because something weird and unexpected happens in a trial. Clearly, double jeopardy is not applied like how you see it on TV and in the movies. In the movies, they imply the rule is that there can never ever be a second trial for the same offense. We know that's not true, and it's not that simple. We see second trials all the time in this business. The point is that courts are not just going to apply double jeopardy mechanically without thinking about what the heck happened and without thinking about the underlying rationale and principles we want to advance.

In regards to this sick prosecutor case, if we get explicit about what we are worried about it would be this: "We don't want the state, with all its resources, to be allowed multiple attempts to try and convict this guy."

We want to restrain the state by not letting it rearm itself nor allow it to strengthen something that it probably never should have begun. This is the main concern and saying it just a little bit differently allows us to see that it falls in line with the first principle. The state should not get a new opportunity to prosecute a case they would have lost. Additionally, we don't want to give defendants a windfall in mistrials where something weird and unexpected happens. Double jeopardy shouldn't be allowed to function as a sword preventing the prosecution of a defendant who would normally and otherwise be subject to prosecution.

In the realm of a mistrial situation, the double jeopardy analysis turns on these competing interests. We don't want to reward the state with a new trial if their case sucked, but we don't want to give a windfall to defendants just because something weird happened to cause the mistrial. Interestingly, the Illinois Criminal Code has a section that addresses this scenario. Let's take a look at it to see if the section captures the ideas we've been talking about here. 720 ILCS 5/3-4(a)(3) says:

> "A prosecution is barred if the defendant was formerly prosecuted for the same offense, based upon the same facts, if that former prosecution: was terminated improperly after the jury was impaneled and sworn…"

The section is saying no retrials if the first trial was terminated improperly. The magic words obviously being "terminated improperly." Super simple to see that this idea is entirely consistent with the way we have framed the problem above.

Now we can begin to roll up our sleeves and begin to think about the rules for allowing a second trial after a mistrial in an initial prosecution.

First of all, if the defendant is the one making the motion for the mistrial, clearly, he is not worried about winning the case. Agreeing to a mistrial puts to bed the idea that the defendant was marching toward a not guilty or an acquittal.

If the defendant is sitting there and legitimately thinking, "I'm going to win this thing," there is no way he's agreeing to a mistrial. So that's the first thing, and we can call it a rule:

> If the defendant is agreeing to a mistrial,
> then a second trial is appropriate.

In order to prevent a second trial, we have to start with a defendant who is not asking for nor agreeing to the mistrial.

The case law then asks, assuming we have a defendant who didn't ask for the mistrial, "was the mistrial warranted by manifest necessity?" That term "manifest necessity," was created by judges trying to wade through these issues, but you can see right away what they mean by that.

They are trying to find a balance between preventing ill-advised prosecutions and the defendant winning a complete dismissal (the public has a right to see that wrongdoers get prosecuted). The term they came up with was "manifest necessity."

The task of the trial judge is to determine if the mistrial was "manifest necessity." If it was, we are all going to have another trial. The court also lists twelve factors that it considers when making its decision. I'll list them here, but you'll get the most use out of them if you think about them through the lens of the competing interests we're talking about here.

The more it looks like the defendant is on his way towards an acquittal the less likely the mistrial is going to be seen as a "manifest necessity". If he was jumping up and down hollering that he does not want a mistral because he wants this jury to reach an acquittal, it's going to be hard to say a mistrial is a "manifest necessity." Double jeopardy should kick in to prevent a mistrial. The more it looks like something weird, random, and uncontrollable happened, even if it's 50-50 that the defendant would win, the more likely it is that the court is going to say there was a "manifest necessity" for the mistrial and is going to allow the retrial.

Using this as your filter, the following are the twelve factors considered by the courts when deciding whether or not to allow a second trial after an initial trial has ended in a mistrial.

> (1) the difficulty was the product of the actions of the prosecutor, defense counsel, or trial judge, or was the product of events over which the participants lacked control;
> (2) the difficulty could have been intentionally created or manipulated by the prosecution to strengthen its case;
> (3) the difficulty could have been "cured" by an alternative that would have preserved the trial's fairness;

(4) the trial judge actually considered the alternatives to a mistrial;

(5) a subsequent conviction would be subject to reversal on appeal;

(6) the trial judge acted in the heat of the trial confrontation;

(7) the trial judge's decision rested on an evaluation of the demeanor of the participants, the "atmosphere" of the trial, or any other factors that similarly are not amenable to strict appellate review;

(8) the trial judge granted the mistrial solely for the purpose of protecting the defendant against possible prejudice;

(9) the evidence the State presented, prior to the mistrial, suggested a weakness in its case (e.g., a witness failed to testify as anticipated);

(10) the jurors had heard enough of the case to formulate some tentative opinions;

(11) the case had proceeded so far as to give the prosecution a substantial preview of the defense's tactics and evidence; and

(12) the composition of the jury was unusual.

If you ever find yourself having to use these factors you know you have the best lens with which to evaluate them. Aren't you wondering what the appellate court did in this case with the sick prosecutor? If you've been reading carefully, you probably have a "gut" feeling on how it went.

The court ultimately conducts all the weighing and balancing we've been talking about and says the judge in this case really didn't know exactly when that prosecutor was going to come back to finish the trial. The jury would have been out three days before there was even the possibility that they would start up again. Under this kind of uncertainty, the trial court was justified in finding a "manifest necessity" for the mistrial. The retrial is therefore proper.

The goal for us is to have these fundamental ideas, principles, and concerns so rooted in our brain that they become automatic. In the future if you find yourself in a situation where you are looking at a mistrial or a double jeopardy problem you will have the right tools to begin to evaluate the problem. You'll be able to probe the right questions, conduct the right analysis, and move closer to your strongest arguments.

PEOPLE V. KIMBALL

One interesting aspect of the double jeopardy question after a mistrial is that the "weakness" in the state's case is just one factor to be considered. It's not as simple as just looking at the strength of the state's case and making a decision. This makes sense.

Many times the judge may not have a good idea if the state had a good case, especially if the thing causing the mistrial happened early. Every instance has to be considered individually and separately. There won't always be an easy answer. Sometimes the prosecution's motives may be entirely unknown, and sometimes the judge may be the sole lawyer driving the mistrial. Anything can happen.

Let me finish up this discussion on double jeopardy with a look at a final case that was released that raised these issues. It's another mistrial setting, so none of the earlier discussion will go to waste.

This time it's *People v. Kimball*, 2017 IL App (2d) 160087 (September). I recorded my summary of this one in episode 398. I was a much calmer guy by this point. Listen below and check for yourself:

https://IllinoisCaseLaw.com/398

By this point, we are all seasoned pros with this double jeopardy issue. In regards to mistrials, we can restate the rule from the above discussion this way:

> "A prosecution is barred after a mistrial if the defendant's trial was terminated improperly after the jury was impaneled and sworn in. If the defendant agrees with the mistrial then double jeopardy does not prevent a new trial. And a second trial is only possible if there was a manifest necessity for declaring the mistrial."

This case was different in that it involved a deadlocked jury. The defendant was on trial for sexual crimes against a minor. The victim was 11 years old when she testified. The defendant denied the allegations, and there was really no other evidence. The victim made different substantive statements every time she spoke about it, so naturally the jury paused before going to a straight conviction.

The jury sent a note back to the judge informing her they were at an impasse and felt deadlocked. They told the judge they weren't going to be able to come up with a verdict everyone agreed on. In those situations, for the defense, those are "red alert" and "hair on fire" moments because they clearly signal the possibility of movement toward an acquittal.

Minimally, this signals there are problems with the case. Some of the jury members are having problems with aspects of the state's case. A prudent and aware defense attorney should be on guard against any early attempts to shut this thing down.

This might be the exact jury the defendant would want to come to a full deliberation on his case precisely because they could come back with the not-guilty. It doesn't mean that they will definitely come back with the not-guilty, anything could still happen, but this might be his best shot at an acquittal. The note said:

> *"Dear judge, after deliberating for 5 hours and despite our best efforts we are at an impasse."*

The judge gathers the attorneys and the parties into the courtroom to inform them of the note. The judge shows it to the attorneys and then tells them that this isn't actually the first note. At one point, the jury wanted to see the video of the child's interview, so everyone gathered in the courtroom so the jury could see it. Shortly after that, they first told the judge they were at an impasse. The judge said he didn't call the attorneys to inform them of this because she thought she could just handle it. She had the bailiff instruct them that they should continue deliberating. Now that the attorneys were informed of what happened, they needed to decide what to do with this new written note.

The attorneys decided to bring the jury back out to communicate with the foreman. They wanted to figure out how bad the deadlock actually was. They wanted to know if with more time they could get a unanimous verdict. They brought the jury out. The judge asks the foreman if more time would result in a verdict? The foreman replied that they had been deadlocked for a good part of the day. He estimated it's been $4^{1/2}$ to 5 hours that they have had the impasse and butting heads. He said some numbers have changed here and there but they've been stuck at the same spot for the last 3 hours. The court suggested that maybe a break would be helpful. What if they let everyone go home for the night, and in the morning they could begin again. The foreman said he didn't think it would do any good. They let the jury go back to the jury room, and the parties stayed in the courtroom with the judge. The attorneys and the judge still needed to figure out what they were going to do.

The prosecutor and the defense attorney were asking the judge to give the jury the *Prim* instruction and have them keep deliberating. The state suggests the *Prim* instruction, and the defense attorney agreed with it and seconded the motion. Defense counsel said to *Prim* them, let them go home and have them come back in the morning to deliberate some more.

The judge tells the attorneys that she was fearful that if they forced them to deliberate some more that they would all just get really angry. She tells them that she's heard some very loud voices coming from the jury room for a while now, and she thought it would be futile to *Prim* them and to require more deliberation. Therefore, the judge declares a mistrial and excuses the jurors.

The question for us now is whether or not there was manifest necessity for a new trial? Will double jeopardy prevent a new trial?

One of the reasons why I like this case is that it gives us a great opportunity to explore the issues deeply. All these cases have allowed us to do that. The rules and the standards are always in the cases.

The rules are there, waiting for us to capture them. What's exciting is that the same material, the same cases, can help us figure out what we would do if we were confronted with similar circumstances. Because you are reading, listening, and thinking about this you won't be caught with your pants down when you see this in court. You will already know what to do. You will have a mini formula and protocol that springs into action. It's in there and just has to spring into action when the right trap is set. It's a reaction rather than deliberation.

In the heat of battle of a trial you are lucky if you remember anything about the law. The fact that you can even put together a sentence is actually pretty remarkable. What you are doing is reevaluating the case from your perspective, like a backseat driver. Make an active effort to determine what you would have done had you been the attorney in the case. What's another way this could have unfolded? What would you have done differently? Would you have known to do this or that?

If you have thought about these questions beforehand, you're going to be better positioned when the crap is hitting the fan in a real trial. If you are doing any amount of jury work, you will see a jury coming back and they are at an impasse. You better believe that's going to happen to you.

From the prosecutor's perspective, what should they have done or could have done differently? Remember, they want to retry this thing.

Also, if this really is a dog of a case, it can't get better, and they just want to get it over with, they may want to push towards a not guilty verdict faster. But if it looked liked the judge was leaning towards the mistrial, and the prosecution did want that second bite of the apple, they could have asked the court something like:

"Judge, I just want to be clear if this mistrial is by agreement?"

Now, that is not a traditional thing to ask in court in the middle of trial. Defense attorneys are used to being asked if continuances are "by agreement."

It is possible some defense attorneys will acquiesce to the mistrial. If you are a prosecutor who has your wits about you, you can ask the question. A defense attorney who is blind to double jeopardy concerns or just hasn't thought all this stuff through may answer affirmatively. It may not matter what they have been arguing and what their prior position has been, if they are asked out right, "Hey are you agreeing to this mistrial?"

Either due to ignorance or just out of habit they may say, "Yes, we agree." If they are not ready for the question, and they answer it in the affirmative, it's a checkmate for the prosecution. They just bought themselves a second trial. Those who know the most get the most. This is just one of those great examples.

Obviously, defense attorneys who are reading this and get asked that question are going to know to tell the judge,

> "Heck no. We ain't agreeing to no stinking mistrial judge. We want this jury to finish deliberating."

It's going to be those attorneys who are not prepared, who have not thought through these issues, who get caught flat-footed in court.

I'm not saying the prosecution did anything wrong in this case. They were clear they wanted the *Prim* instruction and wanted the jury to keep going at it, but the judge was not going to give it to them. Their hands were tied at that point. They could not control that the judge was going to have an *ex parte* communication with the jury beforehand and couldn't predict its influence in the judge's decision to declare a mistrial.

Asking this question is just our way of backseat driving this thing and using the case for our own selfish training. The prosecution loses nothing. It's free to ask, "Hey judge, are they agreeing to a mistrial? Can you just ask the defense?"

They can just ask and live with the results. Either way, they are no worse off.

On the defense side, again, we are not saying the defense attorney did anything wrong. They asked for the *Prim*, they wanted them to go home, and they were clear they wanted them back in the morning deliberating. Maybe they left a little window for the other side to argue that they didn't fight strong enough for continued deliberation.

A defense attorney who has thought of that particular vulnerability and is well-schooled in double jeopardy fundamentals is going to want this jury to finish the deliberating and reach a verdict.

Not only is that the right position that will allow the attorney to later make a claim against a second trial, also this attorney will know that this may be the only jury that is likely to acquit his client. It's these guys. It's these men and women right now that are saying they are deadlocked. If this is at the forefront of the defense attorney's mind, it will put to bed any arguments or notions that the defense acquiesced to the mistrial or didn't fight strong enough.

These attorneys are going to let the judge know in clear and concise terms that they want this jury to come to a verdict. When it's clear that the judge is leaning towards a mistrial, these attorneys will make their intentions clear, hypothetically, with words like:

> "Judge, I don't want to make you angry. You are going to do what you think is right. I don't want to jump up and down and cause a scene here. But our position is that this jury

should be allowed one way or another, either today or tomorrow, to reach a verdict. Let them finish their deliberation process. They are saying they are at an impasse, and they are deadlocked. However, your Honor knows more than any other that juries say that all the time, they get *Primed*, and in an hour they come back with a verdict. That's our position."

The attorneys who have practiced a version of this line in their own head and have thought this issue through before the heat of the moment, will know what to do when confronted with a deadlocked jury.

What's the outcome in this case? On appeal, the defense had to respond to the argument that they agreed with the mistrial. The accusation was that they laid down and didn't really fight it at all. The reviewing court said it was clear what they wanted. It was obvious the mistrial was driven by the judge. Sure, the attorney didn't say anything at that point, but right before that he was asking for the *Prim* instruction and wanted further deliberations. This was not acquiescing to the mistrial.

On the surface, we are looking at what happened here and asking whether or not the mistrial was a "manifest necessity". If it was, then there can be a new trial. If the mistrial was not a "manifest necessity," then double jeopardy kicks in to prevent a second trial meaning the defendant cannot legally be charged again for this offense. The defendant would have to be discharged and allowed to go home.

We have all the same 12 factors at play here that we discussed earlier. The appellate court said it was clear that the *ex parte* conversation with the jury precipitated the declaration of the mistrial by the judge without the judge considering other alternatives.

There was no real reason why the jury could not have been given the additional *Prim* instruction and left to deliberate. If you go back and look at the factors you can see that many more were at play and most tended to lean against a finding of "manifest necessity." The reviewing court said the defendant was robbed of his opportunity to ask for the *Prim* instruction the first time the jurors reported they were at an impasse.

I've been talking about the *Prim* instruction and haven't gone too much into it. Basically, when you get jurors that begin to report they are deadlocked or at an impasse the *Prim* instruction can be given to encourage further deliberation. There is no flat rule on when to give it other than when the impasse is first reported. This can happen 2 hours, 12 hours, or 24 hours into it. I guess there is such a thing as using *Prim* too early. You wouldn't want to give it with all the original instructions because you wouldn't have a lever to pull when they do start reporting an impasse. So, generally the practice is to hold back on the *Prim* instruction until it becomes clear the jury is butting heads.

The reviewing court noted that the impasse here was only 3 hours old. If you factor in lunchtime and administrative time, they were only at it for 3 hours. That's not a lot of time.

The judge's concern with the jury's agitation and anger is not an appropriate factor to consider when trying to determine the presence of "manifest necessity." An emotional atmosphere and a heated discussion are not necessarily bad, and it doesn't necessarily mean the jury will forever be hopelessly deadlocked. To the extent the judge was worried about them being upset or angry, well, that was an error. A judge has much more to worry about than keeping the jury happy.

In the end, the *ex parte* communication weighed heavily against the finding that this mistrial was a "manifest necessity." The judge had other things he or she could have done, like let them keep deliberating. The final holding from the reviewing court was that double jeopardy must step in to prevent the second trial.

This case reminds us that double jeopardy concerns have to be on everybody's mind, including the judge, when a court is flirting with a mistrial. The ideas mentioned here have to be front and center and play a part in the analysis and in figuring out the decisions and positions you will take. No easy answers, but the attorneys who have thought about it, and the judges who are versed in the issue will be more likely than not to handle the issue best.

FINAL TIPS ON LITIGATING DOUBLE JEOPARDY ISSUES

One more thing before I wrap-up this section on double jeopardy. There may very well be cases where defense attorneys are asking for and wanting a mistrial.

Nothing in this section should be read to mean that attorneys must always object to a mistrial in order to win a double jeopardy claim. Sometimes an error is so damaging to your case it may practically guarantee a conviction. In these situations, all this double jeopardy talk goes right out of the window. This business of ours requires you to remain knowledgeable but flexible. The best response in your client's interest will depend on what's happening.

Finally, double jeopardy concerns have been in our criminal justice system a long time. There are cases on the topic going back since forever. This handful of cases I discussed were released by the Illinois criminal court system while I was producing the Premium Nuggets Podcast.

Obviously, I read about double jeopardy in law school. But it wasn't until I had the time to digest and report on these cases that I could make the connections required for deeper learning and understanding. In law school, they don't teach you what to "say" about double jeopardy or what your litigation position should be when you're in court.

When this appears in the heat of trial or a heated motion, the attorney has a limited amount of time to devote to the case law. In these moments you usually are just scanning the cases looking for the "rules," the applicable court standard, or the black letter law, so you don't sound like an idiot.

The listener to the podcast is able to digest these cases, slowly taking in the fundamentals in one case and reinforcing them in the others. Without the stress of battle, you are able to compare the facts of the cases and their outcomes. This, in turn, develops a deep-rooted sense for the "rightness" of the decision.

SECTION EIGHT: SURVEILLANCE PRIVILEGE

I picked one more area of law with an accompanying audio episode to illustrate the value in audio law learning. I've been trying to pick fundamental concepts that have real courtroom consequences for the parties.

This last area of law we'll be discussing is not grandiose or fundamental but can pop up in any Illinois criminal courtroom.

Anytime there is a cluster of cases released on any specific topic that draws my attention, I pounce, dissect, ask myself probing questions, and produce an episode for the listeners. If the area of law is something a litigator is likely to see in court, I waste no time.

PEOPLE V. FLOURNOY

This time it's going to be *People v. Flournoy*, 2016 IL App (1st) 142356 (November). This case will introduce our final topic, the surveillance privilege. Catch the sound file by following this link:

https://IllinoisCaseLaw.com/259

This is a drug investigation. Police are receiving complaints of an open air drug market, and they want to shut it down. They set up surveillance. They have an officer keeping an eye on things and they say they see the defendant engage in a hand-to-hand delivery. The officer says he was about 20 feet away from the defendant. It was daylight. Nothing was obstructing his view. He had a clear line of sight.

The officer insisted it was the defendant he saw engage in the drug transaction. When he sees it, he does not call it in right away, but watches things a bit longer. He sees the defendant walk into an alley where, again, he engages with two women in what appeared to the officer to be additional drug transactions. Money is seen to be exchanged, and the defendant gives the women something. The women then walk away.

It's at that point when the surveillance officer calls in for the arrest to be made by the other officers. The defendant is then arrested, and sure enough, on him they find 8 smaller ziplock bags all containing heroin.

Interestingly though, there is no money found on the defendant. He has no cash on him. The surveillance officer says he never lost visual contact and was sure the man arrested was the man he saw make the deals.

The issue in the case becomes whether or not the state had to disclose the officer's surveillance location. Do they have to tell the defense where the surveillance officer was positioned? Where his station was located? Where exactly he was when he made these observations? There is this thing in the criminal law called the surveillance privilege. It basically says that under certain circumstances the prosecution doesn't have to disclose the surveillance location to the defense. When they withhold that information, we say they have invoked the surveillance privilege.

Since 1998 there have been decisions that say that the rationale for the surveillance privilege is protection of law enforcement. The state could also refuse to disclose the identity of informants so long as it did not interfere with any constitutional rights of the defendant, like his right to confront witnesses.

Everything started with the rationale to protect informants. That's where this idea was born. The rationale is that if you have an informant who is making these observations from, say, their home or their back patio, that's going to disclose the identity of the informant. Then somewhere along the line that idea gets twisted into protecting other police secrets and into protecting these surveillance locations.

The police secrets worthy of protection are things like ongoing police investigations and officer safety. You'd expect police to say something like this, "Judge if we tell this guy exactly where we set up we are not going to be able to shut down that drug market, and it's going to impede other investigations."

Then that becomes a new question. Can the police rely on this kind of police secret to further justify not disclosing a surveillance location to a defendant? There's usually also an argument that police safety may be affected by disclosing a secret surveillance location.

Well let's break down the standards and the tests that have come out of the body of law describing this privilege. As with anything else, it's an obvious balancing test. There is a public interest that takes into account the police goals and secrets along with the desire to protect the identity of informants. That must be balanced against the defendant's right to a fair trial and his right to confront the witnesses against him.

This directly implicates the defendant's right to fair cross-examination. The cases describe some general rules. They are not absolute, but they do help us understand exactly what should happen.

> (1) The surveillance location almost always must be disclosed when there is only one witness against the defendant and it's the witness in the protected area who made the observation in question.

If the entire case rests on one person, whether it's an officer or not, the state is going to be hard-pressed to come up with reasons why that witness's surveillance location should not be disclosed.

If you have a lot of experience in drug cases, all this may remind you of battles between the state and defendants over whether or not the state must disclose the identity of confidential informants. That's not a coincidence.

Similarly speaking there is another general rule that goes the other way.

> (2) When the witness's main observation is not an issue, for example when there are other witnesses who saw the same thing or there is recorded video surveillance of the transaction, then the state likely won't have to disclose the surveillance location.

In practicality, when the state says they want to withhold this information, the judge has to conduct an *in camera* hearing. That just means the judge goes back into his or her chambers with the officer to find out why the police don't want this information disclosed. The judge is also often told outright exactly where the surveillance location was located.

If the judge finds that the police established that the surveillance position was...

> (1) located on private property with the permission of the owner or if
> (2) the officer establishes that the surveillance location is useful and has other utility to the police

then the state is said to have established a *prima facie* case for withholding the information.

The private property element came from wanting to protect informants. If you have private property, it's more likely than not that it was a private citizen or an informant who made the observation. When it's an officer who is standing in a person's property, the inference would still be that the homeowner was colluding and helping the police. In any event, that's where that part of the rule came from.

If the prosecution can establish any one of these two things, then they have made their *prima facie* case. I guess it's also possible that the judge can find that the state did not meet its burden, and it would just end there with a ruling that the state has to disclose the location.

Usually, though, a judge is likely to say the state met its initial burden. But things don't end with just that. There is still a weighing that most go on, and the defendant is given a chance. The burden shifts over to him and he is given a chance to overcome the state's *prima facie* case. What is the defendant going to say to overcome this privilege? What's the standard there? Obviously, he's pointing to his defense and he's commenting on how his defense in the case is now going to be impeded by not having this information.

Courts have set up this dual standard with which to evaluate the defendant's burden at this point. If all this is coming up and being argued for the first time in the middle of the trial, the defendant only has to show that the location is relevant and helpful to the defense or is essential to the fair determination of the cause.

In other words, if the jury's decision is affected by them knowing this, then it must be disclosed. This standard is slightly different if the issue is litigated before trial in a pretrial hearing. The burden then is that the defendant must make a strong showing that the disclosure is "material or necessary" to his defense. "Material or necessary" is different from "relevant and useful." This is how the rules have been set up.

The fundamental error in this case was that the judge didn't give the defendant a chance to overcome the state's *prima facie* case for the privilege. In the *in camera* hearing, the judge was on board with the reasons the police gave for wanting to protect the location. It probably had something to do with other ongoing investigations that would be hampered or something like that. That's just me speculating because we don't know what was said back there. It was error by the court to not have given the defendant a chance to overcome the state's rationale.

The court goes on to say that the state's entire case rested primarily on the testimony of one surveillance officer. One officer was saying he saw the defendant commit these drug deals in an open air drug market. The arresting officers that swooped in, didn't have eyeballs on the guy. It was just that one officer on-the-ready at the surveillance location.

All of this was combined with the fact that the officer was saying he was watching him the whole time with no interruptions. Yet nobody can explain where the money went. This draws into question if they had the right guy.

The fact that the officer did not see the money being dropped or given to someone else was a problem. All of this certainly raised an inference that the officer didn't see what he says he saw. That becomes a central issue in the case. Would this have been relevant and important for the jury to hear and know about? You bet.

The appellate court said that the circumstances seriously call into question the officer's ability to observe the scene from his location. Thus the defendant's need for the surveillance location was great and certainly relevant and helpful to the jury. So the surillance location was required to be disclosed in this case.

The drug conviction was overturned, and the case was remanded for a new trial. The case ended with an admonishing from the appellate court that during these *in camera* inspections it's best practice to take the court reporter back there so everything could be recorded. They didn't have transcripts of what happened back there, and the court said it should be documented to make sure nothing else inappropriate is being discussed.

We don't want cops going back there telling the judge that the defendant is a slime ball and a known dealer. It's kind of important to know what exactly is being said. And the reviewing court can't judge if there really was a *prima facie* case raised if they don't know what the heck was said.

Beware the open air markets, you never know who's watching you.

IN RE MANUEL

For fun let's look at another surveillance privilege case to make sure we got all the right principles. This time it's *In re Manuel*, 2017 IL App (1st) 162381 (January). 9 minutes of audio bliss on this case can be heard below:

https://IllinoisCaseLaw.com/292

In this case, the officer was saying that for 20 minutes he was on binoculars watching the defendant and his friends. They were standing over on the viaduct over the roadway flashing gang signs at cars driving under the underpass. In the officer's opinion this was distracting to the drivers, creating a dangerous situation that could cause an accident.

The officer then goes to the park where these juveniles have moved to. Defendant is there with his friends. The officer pulls the defendant out of the group of youths and arrests him. He is searched, and he has a gun on him. He is charged for having the gun and is never charged with the reckless conduct the officer says he was investigating. He's a minor, so he's not allowed to have a gun. He was adjudicated a delinquent on the gun charge.

The fact that the state was going to claim a surveillance privilege did not get litigated pretrial. This comes up in the middle of the trial. In fact, it was during the officer's cross-examination when the issue first comes up. The officer was testifying about what he saw when the defense cross-examines him with questions like, "Where did you see all this from? Where exactly were you located?" That sounds like a pretty reasonable cross examination question. It's the officer who invokes the surveillance privilege himself by refusing to answer the questions. It's at that point when the state speaks up to tell the judge they are claiming the surveillance privilege, and they don't have to disclose the officer's location. The prosecution settles on an officer safety argument for not disclosing.

This is one of those areas where maybe all of the attorneys had heard of the surveillance privilege but were not particularly keen on the subject. Certainly, nobody prepared arguments on behalf of or to defend against the privilege. The judge has the *in camera* inspection with the officer and the prosecutor but excludes the defense attorney.

Again, we don't know what they talked about because none of the discussion was put on the record. When they all come back out, the judge tells the defense attorney that the privilege applies so the officer doesn't have to reveal his exact location. The defense, however, was going to be allowed to go into some limited areas on cross. They get into the total distance, the lighting conditions, whether there were obstructions, and that sort of thing. The defense attorney objects and this becomes the primary issue on appeal.

Well, we can see from the facts that the state's case depended entirely on just one witness who was saying he saw what he said. The entire case rested on this one person. The defense certainly was challenging the credibility of the witness and calling B.S. on the observations. Clearly, the ability to see the overpass from the officer's location is relevant to the credibility of his testimony.

This case highlights the general rule that when the case against a defendant turns exclusively upon the uncorroborated testimony of one witness who conducted the surveillance, disclosure will almost always be required. In other words, just tell them where the heck you were standing when you saw what you say you saw.

The ruling here, unsurprisingly, was that the trial court abused its discretion by allowing the state to withhold the officer's surveillance location from the defense. As practitioners, we should make sure we are familiar with the rules around the surveillance privilege because it's something the officers know about. It could come up the way it did here. It could be the officers who have been to a seminar or some training where they talk about the surveillance privilege. It could be the officers themselves who start invoking the privilege and refuse to answer questions.

There are thousands of narcotics officers out there who know the term and who come into court thinking they don't have to tell the defense jack crap about where they had set up surveillance. These officers go into court, and they start making their own objections. Jeez, the attorneys better step up to make sure the law is being applied correctly.

The officers just know the term. They don't know squat about making a *prima facie* case, about how the *in camera* questioning should go down, and they don't think the defendant has a chance to rebut the court's finding. None of that. They don't know or care about these details.

This court also took issue with the way the *in camera* inspection went down. The case does a good job of filling in the details on how the *in camera* inspection should be conducted by the judge. *In camera* inspection should mean the judge takes just the officer into his chambers for questions with a court reporter. No one else.

If the judge were handling a package mailed to him for *in camera* inspection, the judge would go into his chambers with the package and wouldn't have the attorneys back there helping him decipher a package of documents. No. If the prosecutor is going back there, then the defense attorney should be allowed to go back there as well to ensure no off-topic matters are discussed.

All the judge needs to know from the officer is where the heck he was standing, what's the location, and also why they are claiming the privilege. The judge's only role is to see if the reason stated by the officer raises the *prima facie* case.

So this decision does a good job of saying that the only person allowed to go back there with the judge is the officer. And for crying out loud, take the reporter as well so everything said back there can be transcribed, sealed, and made a part of the permanent record. That's the right way to do it.

PEOPLE V. PALMER

We're really flying through these later cases. When you see enough cases on a topic and you've given each case their due attention, eventually you internalize the basics.

In regards to the surveillance privilege, there is a protocol and a procedure with clearly laid out rules that eventually get memorized and engraved in your head. *People v. Palmer*, 2017 IL App (1st) 151253 (November), is the next case where the surveillance privilege issue came up. More likely than not if you are on top of this issue and aware of all the moving parts, you're likely to be the smartest attorney on the case on this issue. Read or listen, it's totally up to you. To listen, go here:

https://IllinoisCaseLaw.com/431

Again, this time the issue is sprung on the defense attorney in the middle of trial. It's a drug deal case. The officer is saying he was running surveillance, and he saw the defendant commit three deliveries.

He had him arrested. He dropped some packets of heroin that were picked up by the police, and he had some money on him. It's during the cross-examination of the officer when the defense attorney is getting into the exact location when the privilege is invoked.

The officer does answer some preliminary questions dealing with the total distance, whether it was indoors or outdoors, if there were obstructions, and that type of stuff. But when they get to the question on where exactly he was located, the prosecutor objects claiming the surveillance privilege.

The judge conducts the *in camera* inspection with the officer. It all gets recorded and sealed until the appeal. Because I read the opinion, I as well as you, now know the officer's exact location when he was making the observations described in this case. So, I'm about to disclose a state secret here and announce it to the world: He says he was in a vacant property where there was ample vegetation. That's it. That's the big secret.

He said he needed to get on his knees to see past, over, and through the vegetation using binoculars, and that's how he is able to conduct the surveillance in this case.

The ruling at the trial turned on the fact that the officers wanted to use the location to run other surveillance operations and to make more cases. So the trial judge ruled that the surveillance privilege did apply because there was a state secret which, if revealed, could actually lead to officer safety concerns. The defense attorney is jumping up and down saying something along the lines of, and totally paraphrasing here,

"What is so secret about that? Still, I have a right to cross-examination. My main issue here is that he didn't see what he is saying he saw, and that he physically couldn't see anything from his vantage point. So how are you not going to let me get into that?"

By now we should all have an outline or a venn diagram in our heads featuring all the main legal points defining the surveillance privilege. I know you know this, but all together now, class, in your head, we know that: Everything began with the informant's privilege, which is a statutory thing located at 735 ILCS 5/8-802.3. This is the area of law that allows the state to protect the identity of its confidential informants.

I only mention this because this is what got morphed by judges into what we now call the surveillance privilege. The state has the initial burden of making a *prima facie* case that follows the following guidelines:

(1) This surveillance location occurred on private property with the permission of the owner. Remembering where the privilege came from can be used to help you remember this first prong of the state's burden. The private home thing is all about protecting the identity of the homeowner who is kind of acting like a police informant by allowing the police to use their property to combat crime. The home owner is not giving up information like a traditional informant but there is still an interest in protecting the home owner. That's where

number one comes from. By the way, that's almost never the reason why the surveillance privilege is raised in court.

(2) It's going to be the second prong that is the most common reason for raising the privilege. The second prong requires the surveillance location be in a useful place, so useful that the utility of which would be compromised by disclosure. This prong is saying there is something the state will lose if they have to disclose the surveillance location. That usually means one of two things:

> (a) Officer safety issues or an ongoing investigation that would be hurt by disclosing the location or
> (b) If there is not an ongoing investigation there may plans in the future to run more surveillance operations, then the state's interests can be compromised.

This *prima facie* case requirement works like the rest of them do. If you know it, you can defend against the use of the privilege. It's your job to enforce the *prima facie* case. If it becomes glaringly obvious that the stated rationale for the privilege doesn't meet any of these requirements, you might be able to knock this thing out before it gets started.

There are two general rules of thumb we can use to help make sense of all this. If there is no question about a surveillance officer's ability to observe because there is other contemporaneous evidence like video or other witnesses, then in those cases disclosure of the exact surveillance location is likely not going to be required. The state wins.

Also, if for whatever ever reason, the defense is just not challenging the observations because it's not an issue they are contesting, that's when the surveillance privilege will prevail. This is still assuming the state has met its initial burden. Sometimes this rule may get cited by a prosecutor as the reason to invoke the privilege without making the required showing that the privilege even applies. They may just jump to the fact that the defendant is not challenging the observations. They may try to invoke the privilege by saying, "So we don't have to disclose the location, Judge, if they are not contesting the issue, the case law is clear on that."

Well, the case law is not clear on that. This would be a misstatement of the law. This general rule only applies if the state first establishes the private property thing or has outlined a state interest in keeping the secret. That has to happen first.

We call these rules of thumb, but it's still really a case by case analysis and balancing of interests. There is language on these rules of thumb out there that could get thrown at you. You just gotta make sure everyone is following the correct order of events. These are the basic foundational things that should instantly come to mind when you first hear of the surveillance privilege making an appearance in your case.

There is a little twist here, a significant little twist you need to know about. The case law is also quite clear that the defendant's ability to overcome this privilege, exactly what they need to establish to overcome the state's burden, depends on when the privilege comes up.

The cases point out that it matters when when the challenge is first raised. If the issue is raised before the trial the defense can overcome the state's showing by establishing that the defense's need for the information is "material or necessary" to the defense. The information must also outweigh the public interest in keeping it secret..

The key terms being that it has to be "material or necessary" to the defense. However, if the prosecutor is claiming the privilege for trial, then the defendant can overcome this burden if he can establish that he needs to know the information because it is "relevant and helpful" to his defense. The key terms there being "relevant and helpful" to his defense. I think the idea with these changing burdens is to require a slightly lesser burden on defendants for trial where constitutional concerns would be the greatest. The reason for this difference is not really explained in the cases.

What's the outcome in this case? Well the reviewing court starts from the beginning and lays out the structure of the law the way I outlined it above, and then they went through it. Did the state make their *prima facie* case? Well, I guess, yes. They got back there and said that although there is no active investigation, from time to time in the future they may want to go back there and see what else is going on, so it's more likely than not that they will be running more investigations from that location.

Alright. That's what they said. The defendant then gets a chance to overcome this stated rationale. Here, because all this came up during the trial, the defense only needed to establish that knowing the location of the officer when he made his observations was going to be "relevant and helpful" to his defense. It didn't have to be "material and necessary."

Practically speaking, if they meet one of these burdens they likely can meet the other one as well. The cases don't say that, that's just me commenting on how similar these things are. Here the general rule of thumb about one officer testifying and the state's case relying on that witness seems to be applicable.

They are all fighting about whether he could actually see what he said he saw. The evidence is only coming from the officer's testimony, so the rule is that almost always the surveillance location will have to be disclosed. That rule looks like it should kick in and apply. The state interest in this case is likely going to be the same state interest they bring up in your cases. The state is saying they need to keep the officer's surveillance location a secret because the state won't be able to go back and clean up the neighborhood with other subsequent investigations. The defendant's reply was that the fact of the arrest certainly put the entire universe on notice that the police are running drug investigations in the neighborhood. That's really no big secret to protect.

Do people really have to know the exact surveillance location in order for them to be on notice as to what the police are up to? The gig is up man. The state's secret is basically disclosed. The defense was basically saying there really is not a state or public interest in this case. There certainly is nothing so secret here that justifies giving the state the power to limit the defense's ability to cross-examine the officer.

The reviewing court, when it finally did the balancing, noted this was a one witness case. It further held said if they accept that the state had an interest, it was very low and very minimal compared to the defendant's constitutional right to confront the witnesses against him. The trial judge erred when it allowed the state to withhold this surveillance location. It was reversed and remanded for a new trial where the defense attorney is allowed to have a little bit more fun with the officer on cross-examination. Remember, this officer was on his knees, looking through some bushes, with a pair of binoculars. That just sounds weird, doesn't it? I'd certainly have a little fun with those facts on cross.

Again, by now the basic rules and protocols should be engraved in our heads. There is an initial burden to consider, general rules to know about, an opportunity to respond by the defense, a weighing or a balancing that must be done, and we have to take into account when the issue comes up. Does it come up pretrial or in the middle of the trial?

That's important because it establishes the exact standard we will hold the defendant to in overcoming the burden. But hang with me just a little longer. There is one more case to discuss that really lays out how a court should conduct the *in camera* inspection. Then you'll know everything there is to know. If anyone ever springs this on you, you'll know how to react. If you are the one raising the issue, well now you know how to do it and you will sound like you know what you are talking about.

PEOPLE V. JACKSON

Our last example has us looking at *People v. Jackson*, 2017 IL App (1st) 151779 (November). I really sounded smart in this episode.

Listen for yourself, it's only 10 minutes long:

https://IllinoisCaseLaw.com/432

    This time we will focus on what should happen during the *in camera* inspection. Again, officers are doing drug surveillance. Defendant is observed interacting with other people. They see an exchange. The people the defendant was interacting with are stopped, and they had drugs on their person. The defendant is then stopped, and he too has drugs and money on his person. In the litigation, the state reveals that they will be withholding the officer's precise location because they are invoking the surveillance privilege. Before trial, the defense attorney files a motion *in limine* to force them to disclose and it all gets litigated before the trial.

    During the *in camera* inspection what happens is that the judge goes back there with the prosecutor and the officer. The reporter is also back there, but the defense attorney is not allowed to go back there. The prosecutor is the one conducting the questions. We learn that the prosecutor and the detective talk about other things not related to the surveillance privilege. It essentially sounded like trial testimony, like the questions and answers you'd hear in a trial. They don't ever get into the kinds of things the judge would need to know like, for example, why is the location secret? Why don't they feel they need to disclose the location? What's the state interest? Why are they invoking the privilege?

    Second, they don't actually disclose the location to the judge. They never tell the judge where they made their observations from. Since the defense attorney is not back there, he can' ask for clarification. None of this prevents the judge from holding that the privilege is applicable. The judge comes out from the chambers and tells the defendant that there are public safety concerns involved here. The concerns are not laid out specifically, but the judge assures the defense they existed. The judge says that the defendant doesn't need to know the surveillance location in order to represent his interests at trial. The judge did say the defendant will still be allowed full cross-examination on other relevant issues. They can still get into the officer's distance, evaluation, weather conditions, ability to see, but they couldn't get into the exact location. So it's full cross-examination, except for the part that really matters.

This case really highlights what's really happening in these cases. We see the judge grant the state's motion and then kind of throw a little consolation prize to the defense by telling them they can still ask general cross-examination questions on the observations. A lot of judges probably feel that is satisfactory and that they are meeting all the elements. We know now after looking at these cases that there is a lot more to it than just that.

The arguments made by the defense really did center on the officer's ability to see what he said he saw. They got into it on whether or not the officer broke his surveillance. Apparently, he did break the surveillance at one point. They got into the fact that the officer couldn't remember if he used binoculars in the case. How could he know what he saw if he doesn't remember having binoculars? It was getting dark outside as well. The defense was skeptical he could see as clearly as he made it seem, but since they didn't know his exact location they couldn't probe the issue any further.

On the issue of the *in camera* inspection we begin by asking: Who gets to go back there? This does present the dilemma that judges must face. Before they have a chance to rule on whether the surveillance privilege applies or not, they are confronted with having to decide who goes back with him or her into chambers for the officer's questioning. If the defense attorney gets to go back there, then there is no point in doing the questioning *in camera*. The defense attorney may not ultimately be allowed to have the information, so they won't be back there during the questioning. That's the whole point of having it set up as an *in camera* inspection. The idea is to keep it a secret until it's clear it shouldn't be. So the defense attorney and the defendant have no right to be back there. What about the prosecutor?

The prosecutor likely already knows the surveillance location. It's probably not a secret to him or her, so maybe there is no harm in letting them go back with the judge and the officer into chambers. Then we get into serious confrontation *ex parte* issues.

If the officer and the prosecutor both go back there and defendant and the defense attorney are kept out, then you have one side completely back there and the other side completely excluded. That's a big problem.

Just take this case as an example, the prosecutor and the officer got back there and started talking about all kinds of stuff that didn't have to do with the issue at hand. You could say the judge was given a preview of the evidence without any input from the defense. That's just bad and inconsistent with a fair and just system.

So, the rule this opinion highlights is that only the officer, the judge, and the court reporter should go into chambers for the *in camera* inspection. But if you let the prosecutor back there, then you have to let the defense attorney back there as well. The rule is no attorneys or both attorneys. This sounds like a reasonable rule.

Also, the case helps define the exact substance of the *in camera* inspection. What exactly does the judge need to know from the officer? Remember, in this case the officer never tells the judge exactly what his location was at the time of the surveillance. The appellate court said that was a problem. The court needs to conduct a balancing here, so the judge needs to know the location in order to be able to evaluate and balance the state's interest over the defendant's. There should be a very narrow and limited window of information that the officer must tell the judge. The judge should illicit from the officer...

> (1) What the privilege is, that is, the reason why the state is claiming it must be kept secret. What's the state interest they are trying to advance and protect?
> (2) The officer should disclose to the judge exactly where the surveillance position was located so the judge can accurately consider and weigh the interests.

That's it. That's all that should be discussed back there, nothing else should be brought up.

Of course, the reporter is also there documenting everything. The judge comes out and reports the court's findings, and the transcripts of the session get sealed and stored in the file for the appellate court if this becomes an issue.

When the judge comes out, if the decision favors the state, then the judge must give the defendant an opportunity to rebut and overcome the granting of the privilege. It's also possible the judge comes back and finds that the privilege does not apply. That's possible. That never happens in real life, but that's possible.

The judge could find that the surveillance did not occur from a citizen's private property, and maybe the officer doesn't describe a state secret worthy of protection. Maybe the officer gets back there and just says, "Yea, judge we really hate this guy we don't want him or his buddies to know where we were at." If the cop has nothing more, the judge should deny the use of the privilege. Anyway, it's hard for judges to say no to the police, but the defendant still gets a chance to rebut it.

Here, part of the error was that the defendant was never given a chance to rebut the court's finding. The case got reversed and remanded so that the judge could redo the *in camera* inspection correctly making sure to illicit the narrow bits of information the judge needs to know to decide if the privilege applies in the first place. The error was that the judge did not elicit from the detective the exact surveillance location nor the state interest being protected and advanced.

The judge could not have appropriately weighed and considered all the competing interests if he or she did not have the minimum information he or she needed.

Also, the defense attorney was not allowed into the judge's chambers, which is okay, but here the prosecutor got to go back there, and that introduced another error in the process. On top of that, they got back there and started talking about things that were not relevant to the surveillance privilege issue. The judge granted the use of the privilege and said the magic words that the court knew it had to say, but no real evaluation or weighing took place. So everyone needs to do this one over again.

We know enough about these cases to intelligently guess that when it goes back to the trial level, the defendant should win. It feels like one of those "one witness general rule cases."

Now you know everything there is to know about the surveillance privilege. Sometimes, for subscribers, I create cheat-sheets that have all the important concepts of an issue all in one place. Preferably on one page. I created such a one-page cheat-sheet of the surveillance privilege where I put all the important elements on one page. To add it to your collection just get it on the jump below:

https://IllinoisCaseLaw.com/surveillance-privilege

SECTION NINE: THE LIMITATIONS OF PRINT

Well, the material in this book obviously was not intended to be comprehensive. I chose these limited examples to talk about because they illustrate the value of the Premium Nuggets Podcast.

I thought the examples really highlighted how advancements in your litigation practice could be made through your ears. I mean, I know this was a book and you had to read the material. Duh, that's what you do with books, you read them.

But I'm hoping you had a chance to punch in some of the episodes that were listed in these chapters. I made sure those episodes were available and could be heard by everyone. If you actually read a chapter and also listened to the listed episodes, then you're in the best position to compare the time and commitment each medium demands. And you can compare the the gains and benefits that you got from listening and reading.

On the Premium Nuggets Podcast, many more cases and topics are covered. Anything that is happening in the cases and in courtrooms is fair game. The point is we can cover more on a podcast than we can cover here. It doesn't take long before the limitations of print and the burden of having to read all this stuff becomes obvious.

I'm not against reading. I'm a big fan. I just think active criminal defense attorneys don't need to read the cases if they are able to access the information in some other efficient way. Like, say, a podcast!

Look man, other fields and professions are jumping on this podcasting thing and taking advantage of what the medium has to offer. Why shouldn't Illinois criminal attorneys also be able to take advantage of what this technology has to offer? For example, you can find professional podcasts created exclusively for:

- Teachers
- Professors
- Economists
- Doctors
- Veterinarians
- Nurses
- Dentists
- Accountants
- And there are many more.

I created the Premium Nuggets Podcast because I didn't see why my colleagues couldn't also benefit from having their own podcast. Criminal law litigation in particular is a perfect candidate for audio learning. I wanted to put you on notice that other attorneys are currently using the Premium Nuggets Podcast as the technological liaison between the case law and their litigation practice.

I wanted you to be aware of this effective legal training so you could better control and manage your own courtroom skills and training. After reading this book, I hope you have a better understanding of how audio law learning can help you. Busy, overworked lawyers just don't have the time or the energy to read through dense legal material searching for what they need to know.

There's nothing wrong with making life a little easier. There's nothing wrong with using a little audio technology to make you better at what you do. Your clients, your practice, and your family will be better off because of it. If you want to know more about the podcast I created for Illinois criminal lawyers, then just follow the link below.

IllinoisCaseLaw.com/learn-more

There you can discover more about the podcast and possibly join the waiting list to subscribe. Joining the waiting list is the first step towards becoming a regular subscriber to this audio law learning opportunity. In no time, you too can begin to quickly advance your litigation skills, grow your courtroom experience and begin to have an edge over the competition.

DOWNLOAD YOUR FREE **BOOK BONUS**

Don't forget to download your free bonus podcast episodes. Think of these files as your reward for reading this book. I gathered three episodes that discuss three of the most recent Illinois Supreme Court opinions making the biggest impact in Illinois courtrooms. To get your ears on these audio summaries just follow the link below:

https://IllinoisCaseLaw.com/book-bonus

If you have any questions, comments, or feedback on anything you read or listened to, I can be reached at

partidasam@IllinoisCaseLaw.com

Until we meet again, keep your head up, your ears open and provide wise counsel. The courtroom is a dangerous place, so be careful out there.

www.ingramcontent.com/pod-product-compliance
Lightning Source LLC
Chambersburg PA
CBHW031416210526
45464CB00005B/1908